And They Came To
ROMA SALEYARDS!

John Gilfoyle

First published in August 2007 by
John Gilfoyle
Roma Queensland 4455

Printed and bound by Watson Ferguson & Company, Salisbury.

ISBN: 978-0-9775513-1-6

Cover Photo:
Roma Saleyards Tuesday 1st October 2002.
Yarding 10,500, Wesfarmers share 6182 including the majority of the red Santa Gertrudis cattle from S. Kidman & Co properties and the creamy Charolais cattle from Consolidated Pastoral "Nockatunga".
Wesfarmers Livestock Team:
Rod Turner, Rob Chapman, Matt Beard & Cheryl Bain.

Photo courtesy Rod Turner, Landmark, Roma.

This book is dedicated to my wife

Lurelle

still the best thing that ever happened to me,

and to all those who ever came to Roma Saleyards

and made it

the greatest cattle selling centre in Australia.

Appreciation

Our first two books **Bloody Agents!** and **Bloody Jackaroos!**
were self-published, meaning we did not use a publisher.
This one is the same.
But that does not mean we did everything ourselves;
far from it. You can't write a book on you own.

In this case we received a lot of help from our printer,
Watson Ferguson & Company who have done all our books,
and also from literally hundreds of people who are
either mentioned or depicted in these pages.

Our sincere thanks go out to every single one of you,
for your stories and your humour
or for just standing and smiling to have your photo taken.
Without you, this book would not have happened.

Thank you very much to one and all.

John & Lurelle Gilfoyle.

Contents

Foreword

Over the past forty years the Roma Saleyards have evolved into something of a cultural and industrial icon for Australian cattlemen and women. The yard has an impressive and colourful history and the Roma community dines out on its status as host of the nation's most dominant cattle market.

At the end of the 2006-7 financial year over seven million cattle had been sold through the yards in forty years at a total value of $2,420 million. When we consider the figure that year of $180 million and calculate the dollars retained in the town through commissions, trucking fees, wages and the like, we begin to understand why this facility is so important to the local community. It is an economic driver of dynamic proportions and we shouldn't be too surprised that astute businessmen have started to look for ways to usurp and divert some of that wealth to their own advantage. In a sense, the Roma saleyard may end up becoming a victim of its own success by generating numbers like these.

Clearly a book could be written about the history of the facility, the vision of its founders and the trends of the cattle and beef industries which have been created and manifested here. A long chapter could also be written on the many personalities and the subtle politics within both the Roma Saleyards Board and the Roma Agents Association, but that could make for heavy reading.

In any case, history is not the forte of John Gilfoyle who does two very simple things and does them well. He listens to people and he writes about people. He meets interesting characters, makes a connection with them and commits their stories to paper. And without doubt it is the people and the way they interact with each other that have made these Roma saleyards what they are today.

Very few cattlemen and people associated with the Australian cattle industry have not at some point done business in Roma. There are the abattoir owners and butchers who are represented by their buyers twice a week; the restockers and feedlotters who know they can only

1. What's It All About?

Bloody Agents! printed in 2005, concludes with these lines:

> *What I remember best about being an agent working at Roma Saleyards is the "vibe" of the place; the vibe created by all the people that make it such a bustling hive of activity and the biggest cattle selling centre in Australia.*
>
> *But it's late in the day; too late to go down that track; too late to start talking about these characters and their exploits – humorous, cunning, nefarious or otherwise.*
>
> *As the auctioneer says: "the hammer's up, it's had it's time!"*
> *The rest will have to wait.*

Thanks for waiting.

This new book is about people, the people who come to Roma Saleyards. The people who send their cattle here, the truckies who bring them in, the agents, the buyers, the stockmen and women, the ladies in the canteen, the office staff, and the visitors and tourists who come from all over the world.

Jack Gleeson was the stock salesman for Elders in St George when I first met him, now he is the General Manager Meat & Livestock for Elders in Adelaide. He has a saying about people:

> *There are three rules we must remember:*
> *1. People are more important than things.*
> *2. People are more important than things.*
> *3. People are more important than things.*
>
> *In that order!*

And with that in mind, this book is written about people.

In these pages you'll find a little bit of history, but it's not a history book. Over a hundred people are directly employed on any given saleday; you will find them in here.

The facility is run by a Board made up of representatives of the two local Councils. That's really all you need to know about the ownership and management of the business so we won't bore you with the details of meetings or the decision making processes.

We'll stick to people; people like Tom and Margaret Tulley from Wallumbilla.

Tom managed "Springvale" Boulia for 17 years before moving to the 'Billa, and he attended all the big race meetings at Boulia, Bedourie, Beetoota and even Birdsville till the tourists took over. In 17 years he came to know just about everyone out that way and he still has a few cattle on agistment out there himself.

It's only natural that Tom and Margaret would take an interest in the market at Roma Saleyards, especially when cattle from the far western Channel Country are being sold.

In 2005, the week after *Bloody Agents!* was released, I was walking from the canteen to the yards to be in time for the start of the store sale at 9.00am, when Tom signaled and called out:

"Wait up, over here, there's someone you should meet."

Now I didn't really want to wait up or meet anybody; I had another mission in mind so I waved back and hurried on.

"Hang on John, there's a bloke here you know; come and say g'day."

Well I pulled up, walked over to the vehicle, took a look at the stranger slowly getting out, and Tom said,

"Remember Lyle; Lyle Morton "Roseberth" Birdsville?"

Do I remember Lyle Morton? Is the Pope a Catholic?

Lyle Morton who pulled us out of trouble over twenty times when Fred Keong went out to buy the "Clifton Hills" bullocks in 1964 and it rained we were hopelessly floodbound in conventional vehicles between Birdsville and Betoota?

I didn't recognise the face I hadn't seen for 41 years but I remembered the name and I'll never forget it. In *Bloody Agents!* there's a full account of that disastrous trip; read it and you'll understand why. Without Lyle Morton that day we would still be out there somewhere, little piles of bones in the sand!

Anyway, the other mission was forgotten and the sale started without the market reporter while we all did a bit of reminiscing. I took Lyle's photo and it made my day in 2005 to be able to shake the hand of the man who saved us in 1964.

As it turned out, Lyle now lives at Westbrook, his son Geoff is on Roseberth, and that day Roseberth cattle were in the sale, hence the attendance of Lyle Morton and Tom Tulley.

As I was saying, it's the people who come to Roma Saleyards that create the atmosphere.

Lurelle reads these chapters as they are being written; she corrects the mistakes, improves the grammar and contributes material.

In the middle of the night she thought of how best to summarise this book so she got up and wrote down these words:

"*Bloody Agents!* and *Bloody Jackaroos!* are about real people – this one is about real people too; people in the bush. It engenders a sense of humour, a strong work ethic and a mateship that is unique. It is Australian!"

Now you know what it's all about.

2. In the Beginning

Cattle sales took place in Roma as far back as the 1860s.

Writing about those days in her great book *Kings in Grass Castles,* Mary Durack records that when her grandfather, Patsy Durack of "Thylungra" in the Channel Country between Quilpie and Windorah, wanted to buy more cattle in 1869, "he went to Roma". It follows that there must have been some form of organised cattle trading in Roma at that time.

One hundred years later there were three saleyards operating on the eastern side of Bungil Creek. One set belonged to Australian Estates, another to Queensland Primary Producers Co-operative Association (Primaries), and the third set, "The Blue Yards" were owned by the private agent Dick Condon, who sold out to Winchcombe Carson.

In the fifties, all agents would use the three yards on any given day, with steers in one set, heifers in another and cows and cows & calves in the third. Fat cattle were sold the same day and blended into the yarding wherever there was room. At that time sales were held about once a month depending on the availability of cattle.

A few consignments came in trucks but most were walked in by drovers. A mob would be delivered to one set of yards, split into lines of fats or stores, steers, heifers or cows, and then stockmen on horseback would take them across to whichever set of yards was designated by the delivery agent.

Depending on numbers, up to half a dozen mounted stockmen such as Roy Harms, Charlie Kadel, Bob Isles and Charlie Cosgrove were so employed. Other stockmen in those days included Ken Kavanagh, Norm Harland and Arthur Ferguson.

For the facilities available at the time, it was a good system in that it did work and numbers got up around 1500-2000 head sometimes, but it was labour intensive, inconvenient and time consuming. There had to be a better way.

In 1967, the local Councils, being the Roma Town Council and the Bungil Shire Council, became directly involved and, in consultation with the agents, decided that all three yards would close down in favour of substantial new yards to be erected by the Roma Bungil Saleyards Board for the use of all Roma agents.

Ken Tomkins was the Chairman of the Bungil Shire and a driving force behind the new yards while Ken McGrath was the Mayor of Roma. The first Saleyards Board was made up of selected councillors from the town and shire as well as Tomkins and McGrath and McGrath was elected chairman.

The first sale was held in the new yards on 7th October, 1969.

Parliamentarian Bill Knox, later Sir William Knox, opened the sale. He also auctioned the first lot in the bull ring, a line of Hereford bullocks owned by local butcher Charlie Wedderkopp.

Then it was over to the agents to sell the rest of the cattle, about 1200 head, in the new ironbark selling pens.

Primaries had drawn first sale. The night before, the men were discussing the next day over a few cold beers and Bryan Hickey posed the question as to who would actually auction the first pen.

Arthur Walmsley, the Branch Manager was there, so too George Henderson, Store Stock Manager for Queensland and Bryan was their local Livestock Manager.

"Who'll kick the sale off?" asked Bryan.

"Well," replied George, "I'm the senior man but you're the local bloke; you do the first lane and I'll do the next one."

And so it was that Bryan became the first agent to sell in what is now the biggest cattle selling centre in Australia. Furthermore, at the ripe old age of 81, he's still in Roma and is still associated with Roma Saleyards on a regular basis.

It was a big day; an important day in Roma's history and Bryan recalls the presence of a host of local stock and station agents including Ozzie Frost, Val Harms, John Molony, Ron Armstrong, Kevin Watkins and others.

But wait a minute! Was there another "first" sale? Graeme Thrupp tells me there was.

"There was a Santa Gertrudis Stud Sale before the yards were properly finished and the complex was officially opened. It was held on 25th September 1969.

There were two vendors, my parents Harold & Gwen Thrupp 'Roylands' Surat, and Samuel S. Bassett 'Taloona' Roma, and two agents, Australian Estates and Dalgetys. The legendry auctioneer Dave Watkins came down from Rockhampton to do the selling for both agents; he was acknowledged as the authority on the Santa Gertrudis breed."

So, if you like, Dave Watkins was the first agent to sell stud cattle and Bryan Hickey was the first to sell commercial cattle.

Anyway, with the new yards underway, Val Harms, the manager of Winchcombes, approached Charlie Cosgrove and Roy Harms to be on hand for every sale to receive stock, help the agents with the drafting and paint the fats.

In addition to their other duties Charlie and Roy would also marshal cattle after the sales for the major buyers such as Pat Clarke and Peter Knauer.

I met Charlie in 2007 when he was 77. He told me:

"I was a drover from the age of 16, started at the saleyards in 1955 when I was 25 and gave it away in 1990 when I turned 60.

George Timms was employed to do most of the drafting. He never went back over a pen and when he finished with them they were like peas in a pod. The agents used to get him to do the sales at Quilpie and Charleville as well. He was tops."

Charlie saw many changes and increasing numbers during his 35 years at the yards and he has so many stories to tell he could write his own book:

Roy and I would start the afternoon before a sale. We would go up, make a bit of a camp on the flat near the yards, get things organised, take delivery of cattle that afternoon and during the night and be ready to start early the next day.

We would roll out our swags on the ground and cook up a feed on the fire, enough to do us for breakfast as well.

Eventually they got us a van, an old Bungil Shire plywood caravan that leaked when it rained. We painted a sign on the door 'No.10 Downing St.' and that is what it became known as. If it rained too heavy, and it did rain in those days, we would sneak up into the office and camp out of the wet.

Jo and I were married in 1973 and her mother gave her a Bessemer saucepan for a wedding present. By that time sales were twice a week - stores on Tuesday, fats on Thursdays – so on Mondays and Wednesdays, Jo would knock up a stew in that beautiful big pot, enough for me and Roy for dinner and breakfast, and we would heat it up on the little burner at No.10. It was like staying at the Ritz!

One night while we were camped out, a couple of hundred of Peter Knauer's weaners got out of a wire yard. I don't know how it happened, the gate wasn't busted or anything, someone might have let 'em out for a joke.

Anyway they were well gone before we realised that they had headed off towards town, crossed the Bungil and got about as far as where the Big Rig is now.

We followed them on foot and found them coming back with the pound keeper in one car and a policeman in another car doing the droving.

It was very dark but we got 'em back across the creek and we were coming up past the sheep yards on the train line when the mob split. The car drivers could only see what was in their headlights and they didn't realise what had happened till they got 'em back in the yards and the copper said, "We had more cattle than this?"

Doug O'Sullivan had just come back from a campdraft and he had three horses on his truck so we unloaded them and went looking for the rest.

We got 'em down by Peter Green's on the old Surat road, brought 'em back, gave 'em a count next morning and we were two short, but Gerry Logan found 'em dead where a train had hit 'em down by the meatworks, so the numbers balanced.

Another time when Wally Humphris was buying for Jack O'Hagan, he rang up in a panic to say about a hundred of his bullocks had somehow got out of the trucking yards and he wanted to know if I could go and find 'em.

Well I went down and picked up a couple then kept on riding and found the rest at Blythedale. They were due to truck out at 11.00am and I got 'em back just in time, just as the engine was hooking onto the wagons.

Johnny Bushell came out from Brisbane; he was a buyer for Borthwicks. He had an old International 4-ton truck and I had one too but mine was a bit newer.

Anyhow, Bushell reckoned we should have a race in these trucks and with nothing better to do one morning before the sale, I

7

decided to take him on. The distance was to be from the saleyards back to the grid.

I said to Roy, 'Let's cross the wires in his truck?'

'Don't do that, he'll kill us!'

'Oh, he'll be right.'

Anyway I did, I crossed the wires, so that when it came to racing and Johnny started his truck it went bang! bang! bang! bang! … and the race never got started.

I still don't know to this day whether he knows who did it … but he will when he reads the book!

During the Beef Slump in the seventies when cattle were worth next to nothing, Val came to us and said they couldn't afford two men and would have to put one of us off. We told him it was too dangerous a job for one man on his own but he argued there was no way they could continue to pay the two of us.

Roy and I had a think about it and went back and told him we would both stay on and work for half pay on the understanding they would square up when things came good … and they did too!

To make ends meet, Jo and I bought the newsagency at Maleny and operated that for two years. Jo had some previous experience in the business but I didn't go on it much at all and used to come back to help Roy in Roma every sale; didn't miss one.

I did the same when I was droving. Apart from one time when we up around Cloncurry, I made it back every sale.

There was a truckie unloading cattle; he was full of yippee beans and he couldn't get his truck in right to unload. Roy was there giving directions, trying to help, but it wasn't doing any good and the driver was getting a bit toey.

I was away putting cattle on water so Roy was there on his own and when I come back this fella was just about to get stuck into Roy; he was full of beans and would have done some harm if I hadn't come along.

That's what I was saying, how it can be dangerous for one man to be on his own … in more ways than one!

One fat sale in the late seventies we had 3002 head, all fats. Like everyone else, we were up all night and got pretty tired but after they were sold, we had to paint 'em, with brushes, every single beast –

Andersons Wallangarra behind the head, Borthwicks on the shoulder, Riverstone on the loin etc

Roy and I did the lot on our own but we were buggered by sundown and it looked as though we mightn't make it through to the end.

Doug Kirk, the manager of Estates, came along and encouraged us to keep going; Doug Thomson from Estates was there too. They reckoned we had it beaten and there weren't many more to go, so we battled on and finished just on dark.

Then Doug Thomson came over said, 'You blokes will find a cold carton of beer under that Athel Pine; you deserve it.'

Well that's as far as we got, we were so tired we couldn't even talk."

"How did you get home after that?" I asked.

He laughed. "Don't know. Don't know how, don't know when; it was a long day."

Jo chimed in, "Charlie never used to drink at all till he went to the saleyards."

He wouldn't have been the first to have 'one' after a sale and forget how he got home; after a big sale or a special sale, parties could go all night!

As this chapter was being written, I ran into John Warner who used to own "Rockybank" at Roma.

"How's the new book coming along?" he asked.

"Well, I've made a start; did an interview with Charlie Cosgrove on Monday."

"Charlie Cosgrove, quiet spoken bloke, a real gentleman. Give him my kindest regards."

How many of us will be remembered as real gentlemen?

3. Truckies

In the early days cattle were walked into Roma by the owners or drovers, but times were changing and even in the thirties a few little lots, of say four or five head, came in on body trucks.

One bloke believed in road transport as the way of the future.

Fergus Williams owned a trucking business. He carried produce, bagged grain, wool and heavy machinery but he was convinced he could also handle cattle and sheep.

In 1939 Fergus designed a trailer to attach to his 1936 C-model 6-ton International and took the design to Sargeants Engineering (now ANI-Komatsu) in Brisbane. They built the trailer to his specifications, it was transported to Roma and Ferg built a livestock crate to fit it.

He made it 32 feet long, 8 feet wide, 5 feet 6 inches high, same size as a railway K wagon, with LIVE STOCK TRANSPORT in big letters painted down each side.

Local graziers were skeptical; they reckoned the semi-trailer would break in half. To prove it could be done, Ferg transported the first load for nothing.

In October 1939, he took Alan Campbell's 20 bullocks from "Merino Downs" Roma and unloaded them in the railway trucking yards. The 23 mile journey took less than an hour; ordinarily, it would take two days and two nights on the road to cover the distance.

The 318 miles to Cannon Hill saleyards in Brisbane took 40 hours. A straight run through on the truck could have been done in 15 hours if it were not for the transport legislation of the time.

In the story about that delivery in the Country Life under the headline REVOLUTIONISING STOCK TRANSPORT the paper commented: *A combination of motor transport and express stock trains would revolutionise livestock marketing in Queensland.*

We all know that took a long time to happen, but it was Fergus Williams who gave birth to the concept as far back as 1939!

Fergus retired in 1973. During nearly 50 years in the transport industry he never had an accident, never lost a beast and earned a reputation for service and punctuality.

His family allowed me to read from their collection of albums and scrapbooks that bear testimony to his achievements and to record a couple of quotes from his clients that will give you some idea of how well respected he was.

In November 1962 Ken Johnson "Lenroy" wrote: *Many thanks for your ever present co-operation and first class deliveries,* while a letter from Boyd Brumpton "St Kilda" dated September 1973 reads: *Just a note to say thank you for the courtesy and attention that you gave to us over the years when transporting our stock.*

When I was putting this chapter together in February 2007, Dennis Hickey, one of Ferg's sons-in-law, took me to meet the man himself and I shook his hand.

I had never shaken the hand of a 103-year-old before and I didn't know what to expect, but the hand was firm, the smile friendly, and there was a thrill about being with him and hearing his stories about the transition from horses to horsepower before I was born.

It was a real honour to meet Fergus Williams – a great family man, a pioneer of livestock transport and the first truckie that came to Roma Saleyards.

After the war, that's World War II, motorised transport gradually became more and more common. In the fifties bigger body trucks and semi-trailers were well entrenched in the industry though drovers still handled the big mobs over long distances.

The semis then started towing an extra trailer. The trailers became longer, up to 40 feet instead if the original 32 feet, and trucking pioneers like the North Australia Pastoral Co (NAPCO) developed their own fleet of road trains with Leyland prime movers towing two trailers behind a body truck.

In 1965, Tom Gadsby from Byrock NSW built a unit that took three decks of sheep and towed a trailer that took two levels. That was a real novelty in those days but the big breakthrough came when he converted the three levels for sheep into two levels for cattle. The first double decker!

Today we have the likes of Fergus Williams and Tom Gadsby to thank for the livestock transports that traverse the nation – doubles, B-Doubles, four deck road trains, AB-Triples (5 decks), and the huge 50-metre-long six-decker monsters – which means that cattle from all states of Australia can be sold, and have been sold, at Roma.

There have been a couple of lots from "Rosewood Station" Kununurra, plenty of cattle off the Barkly Tableland and around Alice

Springs, Mavis and Phillip Page, Quamby Angus Stud in Tasmania, have sold through the Roma bull ring on several occasions and Don Kelly reminded me of one consignment from the Kimberley.

Cattle have come from Rob & Jan Flute "Wairuna" Mt Garnet, Malcolm McClymont "Mt Sturgeon" Hughenden, Frank Booth "Cowie" Cloncurry, David Brook "Adria Downs" Birdsville, and from the Sidney Kidman & Co properties throughout the Channel Country and down into South Australia.

In early 2007, while the drought still raged in southern states, we had big numbers out of NSW and Victoria including consignments from Sale, Jerilderie, Coonamble, Wagga Wagga, Delungra, Warialda, Young and Narrabri.

It's usual for cattle to come from the north and buyers from the south, however, on 13th February that year when 4000 head out of a yarding of 8000 came from NSW and John Rae "Moonambil" Coonamble sent in 915 mostly Angus steers, buyers from as far north as Boulia, Winton, Clermont and Springsure were not only present but operating strongly.

At that time southern drovers had mobs on the road looking for feed and some owners, including Guest & Co "Dalman Downs" Narrabri, took advantage of the market to unload stock at Roma that day. Just goes to show the days of the drover are not over yet.

But it goes without saying that truckies brought most of 'em in and took all of 'em home. So let's have a yarn with some truckies.

Peter Green has been carting cattle to Roma yards for over 40 years. He's always had either one or two 22ft body trucks and operates the business in partnership with his wife Janet.

"The trucks have elastic sides," he says, "so we can always load those extra couple they want us to take that won't fit!"

Peter reckons he's never made any money but he hasn't gone broke and seeing that he's only 70 now he's looking forward to the next 40 years. Then he told me this story:

Back in the eighties, the phone rang one night; it was Primaries manager Robert Brown asking me to pick up a load of steers from David Rathie at "Tarawonga".

I went down the next afternoon, wound my way through all the wilga trees and found the yards. The cattle were there, 25 of them, and the permit was made out, all was okay, so I loaded up and took them to the saleyards. When I got there I counted them off. There were 25!

Next morning the agent rang to say they only had 23.

"Couldn't be right," I said. "Counted them myself three times; there was definitely 25 head!"

"There are 23 of the Tarawonga steers here now and we have checked and checked again, we've been all over the yards and all we can come up with is the 23!"

"Well I'll come out and have a look around myself."

There were 7000 cattle there that day, which was a big sale for those days, and there were cattle everywhere. But I knew exactly what they looked like, the age and the size and the breed, and I just kept walking up and down the pens of similar cattle till I spotted them.

The two steers were in a pen of cattle in the Dalgety run!

I got hold of David Rathie, showed them to him and he confirmed beyond doubt that they were his. It didn't take long to sort things out and the cattle were correctly penned before the sale started.

Then David said to me, "Thanks very much; I'll make sure you get a carton of beer for that."

I don't know if he was going to get the carton, or the bloody agent was supposed to get the carton; all I know is it hasn't come yet!

Jim Schefe was born in Roma, in fact his father, Arthur Schefe "Springdale" Roma, sold the first pen of cattle in the "Blue Yards" back in March 1956, and it was Fergus Williams who brought them in on his semi-trailer.

For many years, Jim was also a regular vendor himself and in October 1973 he held the Roma Saleyards record price for a bull at $500.50. The buyer was Fred Keong.

Jim started trucking 23 years ago. Back then he had a 3 ton Toyota that was flat out lifting five bullocks; these days he uses a 7 ton Hino with a 20 foot crate that carries the equivalent of half a deck.

Craig Dillon, Yunta Transport, Yunta SA was here in December 2006 with a load of "Packsaddle" cattle.

"We often come to Roma Saleyards especially with the Kidman & Co cattle from "Quinyambie" he said.

Dr Jim Baker A.M. M.B.B.S. F.R.C.O.G. (Lond.) F.R.A.N.Z.C.O.G. is an unlikely truckie in that really he is an obstetrician.

While practising on Wickham Terrace in Brisbane during the Beef Depression in 1975, he purchased the cattle property "Lighthouse" on the Taroom Road northeast of Roma.

That's how he got involved with trucks!

He found that any time he wanted to move cattle he couldn't get a truck so in 1979 he decided to buy his own, a Mercedes Benz 1418 single axle prime mover with a 36ft Hallmark trailer. Now he was free to cart his cattle whenever it suited him.

But then he found that the neighbours wanted to borrow it and everybody would ring up and ask for the truck just when he planned to use it himself.

This is the story Jim told me:

So I said, "Bugger this! I'll employ a driver," and we rented a house in Roma and started Lighthouse Transport. In 1980, Tommy Grace was engaged to manage the trucking operation and he ran it for 20 years.

As an obstetrician and gynaecologist working in the city but with experience in the bush, I could see a need for these specialist services to be available in far flung country areas, so I put forward the notion of having a "Flying Obstetrician" attached to Queensland Health similar to the already established Flying Surgeon Service. The idea was 'my baby'!

In 1988 the 'baby' was born and I was offered the position.

I chose to be based in Roma and now my various roles were combined in one centre so much so that the accountant described my occupation on my tax return as "grazier, farmer and transport operator with medical interests". I might tell you it was the medical interests that financed the rest!

In those days, truckies were getting a raw deal from the government on all fronts; double decker trailers were considered to be overweight and fines were being issued. The transport operators were not organised as a united body and whether I liked it or not, I was caught up in it all.

Jock Douglas was the Chairman of the Cattleman's Union and he assisted us to convene a meeting of livestock transporters in Roma. A lot of us turned up and another 'baby' of mine, the Livestock Transporters Association of Queensland, was born.

Bruce McIver was elected President, I found myself elected Secretary, a committee was formed and away we went.

Subsequently we pushed the issue of volume loading, which was the concept of a standard sized trailer and crate not being able to be overloaded, and within 12 or 18 months we had it legally established with the Department of Main Roads due, quite frankly, to the assistance of Russ Hinze.

You may recall, he was the Minister for Everything: Main Roads, Police, Racing and Local Government all at the one time; he really knew how to get things done and he was very good to us.

I'll never forget the meeting I had with him in the suite of his hotel during the National Party conference.

I turned up at the appointed time and was ushered into his presence. There was quite a group of dignitaries plus the Director General of Main Roads, Eric Fenger, and Don Lane, who was the Minister for Transport. Anyway there was quite a crowd.

Hinze had the reputation of taking control of such meetings by asserting his authority from the very outset, often quite crudely, and he did so on this occasion.

The person introducing me said,

"Mr Minister, this is Jim Baker the Secretary of the Livestock Transporters Association; Jim is a gynaecologist. For God's sake don't ask him how he got involved with trucks; it's a long story."

In typical fashion, Hinzey looked me up and down, and said,

"Humph, you don't look like a so-and-so gynaecologist!"

In the silence that followed, you could hear the sucking in of breath all around the room. But remembering the stories about the man and realising this could be the quickest ministerial meeting on record, I made the decision to come back.

So I then very deliberately looked him up and down and said,

"Well, you look pregnant!"

Whereupon there was another in-drawing of breath in the room, followed by total silence … then Hinzey burst out laughing.

Within five minutes he was referring to me as "My friend Jim" and 10 minutes later we had volume loading for 40ft standard double deckers approved. The industry has never looked back.

With the Association attracting more and more members we held meetings in Brisbane to coincide with the Truck Show and in the evenings we would host what we called the Bullcarter's Ball.

15

Remember the one when you and John Robbins were our guests at Lennons? There were people dancing on tables but the couple that actually came down was on the dance floor!

It was the Director General of Main Roads, Eric Fenger, and his wife that fell, we laughingly said, "She fell down a pothole", but it really wasn't funny because she suffered a broken ankle. That put a dampener on proceedings for a while.

I attended to the injured limb till the ambulance arrived; they parcelled her up on a stretcher and carted her off to the Wesley, and frivolities resumed.

Back in Roma, when Tommy had a weekend off, I would be on call for the trucks.

Of course I was also on permanent call, 24 hours round the clock, as the O & G (obstetrician & gynaecologist), so I had two mobile phones - the one on my right hip was the Flying O & G Service and the one on my left was Lighthouse Transport.

When a phone went off I had to work out whether to answer "Professor Baker" or "Lighthouse Transport" and as you can imagine, mistakes were made and there were stunned reactions from callers at the other end.

In those days we were doing Consolidated Pastoral's work and carting fat cattle from Roma to Lakes Creek meatworks in Rockhampton. It was not unusual for us to be moving 30 decks out of the saleyards and yours truly would be out there loading trucks on weekends, mud and shit all over me, in the thick of it all, and hoping that I wouldn't suddenly be called to an emergency birth in Mt Isa.

I remember when my wife, Jill, stood for Council. I was trucking, she was handing out "How to Vote" cards and I decided I had better vote, so I went to the booth in my filthy trucking gear stinking to high heaven.

Jill turned up her nose as I approached and said,

"I don't think I can hand you a card, you smell!"

"Well I won't vote for you; I'll fix you."

She handed me a card, she was elected, and Jill became Deputy Mayor of the Roma Town Council.

It was good fun, they were good days.

I'd spend time up at our depot too. Tommy and the drivers would be working on the trucks, changing tyres, and I'd be in there supposedly lending a hand but probably getting in the way, and the boys would be terrified that I would have an accident and get my hands caught in something.

Eventually they'd find some excuse to get rid of me and send me off for parts or a tool, anything anywhere to get me out of the road. I became the gofer. They assumed that I didn't know what was on, but I was well aware they were really looking after me, mothering me, and I appreciated the relationship with them all.

With old age approaching and retirement looming, it was time to move on. The aim was always to retire and reside on the property and that wasn't going to be possible with the trucks, so we sold.

I sold out to an old mate, Ross Fraser, Frasers Transport. We had been friends for 20 years; he was one of our original committee men in the Livestock Transporters Association … and I might tell you it was a very happy and amicable transaction.

"Lighthouse" is on the range with panoramic views …
and so Jim and Jill went up the hill!

Tommy Grace ran Lighthouse Transport for those 20 years. He and his wife Mary then moved into Brisbane and while everyone said, "You'll be back," Tom and Mary are still down there and loving it.

Tom recounts his three most vivid recollections of those days:

"The most amazing experience I had was the fish!" says Tom.

"It was Thursday afternoon, the sale was over and I took a truck out to load fats. I stepped down and there were these fish on the ground, little silvery black buggers about four or five inches long.

I thought some one must've dropped a packet of bait or something but they were all over the bloody place, on the ground, up the ramp, in the lanes, everywhere.

I'd heard of blokes talking about it raining fish but I never believed it could be possible, yet that's what must have happened."

"The most frightening thing was to do with a busload of tourists.

This big coach pulled up and about 40 old people shuffled into the yards to have a look at what was going on. This was before they built that big overhead platform so they were all on the ground.

The visitors were in the lane looking into the pens on either side and we were down the bottom end loading out. Next thing this speary-horned Brahman bullock jumped a fence and headed straight up the lane at full gallop. I could see what was going to happen and feared the worst but I couldn't do anything about it.

Anyway, he raced right through the middle 'em and never hit one. We followed up and locked him in a pen down the far end.

The poor old dears were quite shaken up; I'd rather be doing their cookin' than their washin', and they all left shortly afterwards probably not realising how lucky they were."

"The most embarrassing time was on my birthday.

Mary must have rung someone at the yards during the store sale and told them it was my birthday and suggested that they make a bit of a fuss, get the buyers to sing *Happy Birthday* or something.

Well I'm in the lane following the sale and drumming up a bit of business, Peter 'The Mouse' Holland is selling, and we've just come to pen 20 (that's pen 296 now) when there's this announcement over the loudspeaker that stops the sale.

The voice says, 'We interrupt the sale with a special announcement, an important birthday announcement, it's Tommy Grace's birthday, Happy Birthday Tom, and you are all asked to join with me in signing …'

And he breaks into *Happy Birthday to You* on the mike, and everyone laughs and sings a bit, and they're patting me on the back, and the song is going on and on, and 'Mouse' is getting upset because it's stopped his sale, and I'm getting redder and redder, and everyone is laughin' and thinkin' it's a great joke.

And when I told Mary she thought it was funny too.

I never did find out who did the singing. Keith Kimlin would know because he would have had to turn the speakers on, though he wouldn't tell me, but I've always suspected it was the bloke who's writing this book?

His turn will come!"

Morrie Troy has been trucking livestock for 20 years. Currently, he is the Livestock Co-ordinator for Gilberts Transport in Toowoomba; before that he was with Rural Freighters in Toowoomba and Porters in Roma; and before that he had his own truck.

Morrie attends the sale every Tuesday to arrange deliveries to feedlots at Condamine and the Darling Downs for his clients.

Scott Henry has been working for Curley Transport Cloncurry and Charters Towers for eight years.

"We often get down this way carting northern cattle to the southern works but we come into the saleyards several times a year.

"I've come here with the Brassington cattle from "Corella Park" and the McDonald Holdings cattle from "Devoncourt", but today I'm going the other way, backloading Santa heifers bought by Reg Beauchamp "Stockport" Boulia.

Keith Aisthorpe has been in Roma all his life but only started in the transport business 14 years ago. He drives a 25ft Isuzu truck and does mainly local carrying in a 150km radius, but work from stud sales has taken him as far as Tamworth, Nebo, Rockhampton, Gympie and the Gold Coast.

"The directions to that one were: Go down as far as Dreamworld, turn right, and we're 10km inland from there."

"What have been the highlights so far?" I asked.

"Well a bull kicked back on a gate that broke my nose; I took the dearest bull ever sold in Roma, the $68,000 bull out of the 2005 Heartland Santa Gertrudis Sale, to Tamworth for Moreton Rolfe; I was bogged once, up north of Pickanjinnie, just past "Tantallon", and it took six days to get out; and I've been knocked down by a bullock and had a shoulder reconstruction that kept me off the road for three and a half months.

I'm 65 this year, they say it's time to give it away, take it easy, but I've met a lot of decent people - only a few I wish I hadn't – some have become good friends, and all in all I'm very happy doing what I do, and I'm going to keep on doing it!"

John Butler was born in Roma. "Butts" is the Goondiwindi manager for Frasers Transport, has been since 1985 and he's been on duty at most Roma store sales since then.

In those 22 years he has seen a lot of sales, met a lot of people, handled a lot of cattle and arranged a lot of trucks. When I asked him:

"Do you like coming to Roma?" this was his answer:

Well I find Roma very rewarding. The people here are very friendly, people here are very busy and I've met some very good people here, good people to deal with and good people to mix with socially.

I go to a lot of saleyards and of course this is the biggest, it's the biggest in Australia, and the client base that this place has got is second to none.

But what I especially enjoy are the special sales when the yards are full of top quality one breed cattle whether they be Herefords or Santas or Charolais types or whatever. They are a real sight to see and it's worth coming here on those days just for a look.

Our Roma business is expanding; we've had our own depot here since we purchased Jim Baker's business, Lighthouse Transport, and we are now in the process of setting up a new depot on the land we bought on the western boundary adjacent to the saleyards.

Melissa Jensen runs the show here. We have plenty of girls in the office back home, but Melissa is the only lady that I know actually running a livestock trucking operation.

She is very efficient, gets on well with the drivers and the boss is very happy with the way she manages the business.

Just like every other saleyards, there are characters here at Roma. We've had some ups and downs with 'em over the years, things going right, things going wrong, there have certainly been some laughs, there have been some serious points put across, but we're all still mates and still doing business.

Truckies came up with the nickname "Captain Insanity" to tag one bloke, the man himself Peter "Pluto" Tudor. He's been in the game a lot longer than me and handles a massive amount of cattle. He certainly has his ups and downs but he's one of the great characters of the industry, that's for sure, and we'll all miss him when he's gone.

This place has lost a lot of those great characters, men I looked up to for their professionalism; people like Ross Stewart and Val Harms are lost to the industry forever and will never be replaced.

Ross Stewart was the Primaries manager. I did a fair bit of business with him and I can honestly say he was one of the best I have had to deal with.

One Tuesday sale he gave me a load to cart to Goondiwindi. I was to ring him that night for final instructions and when I did call the Stewarts number I was a bit surprised that the priest, Father Michael Cooney answered the phone.

"I have to relay the very sad news that Ross passed away this afternoon," he said. So he was gone, just like that.

It was certainly a bad day for me, the Stewart family and the whole community, but I'm pleased to see the Saleyards Board saw fit to honour him with a memorial plaque which is still there on the wall.

One of the funniest men I ever had anything to do with and one of the biggest characters is Brian Morrissey - heart of gold, tough as nails, calls a spade a spade, and his word is his bond.

Then there was Pat Clarke, a gentleman. He attended Roma sales religiously every Tuesday and we carried a lot of cattle for Pat.

When Frasers first moved to Goondiwindi they bought a paddock off Pat to establish a depot and that's where we still are today. We did a lot of business with the Clarke family over the years.

It was time for Butts to move on so I finished up by asking, "Well where to now, what's the plan for the rest of the week?"

I left Goondiwindi this morning and I'll head out now and leave this lot to Melissa. By tonight I'll be in Blackall, do the Longreach sale tomorrow, the Blackall sale on Thursday, there'll be other jobs in the paddock to tie up as well but I should get back to Gundy some time on Friday or Saturday. Last week I didn't get home at all!

I've been doing that for five years but I wouldn't be doing it if I didn't enjoy it. Some days it gets a bit monotonous but the good part of it is the people you deal with and the characters you meet.

They make it all worthwhile!

Melissa Jensen manages Frasers Roma Depot. She is one of very few women on the action side of the livestock transport business, but seems to thrive on the life.

It can be a bit stressful, especially late on a Tuesday night trucking out after a big sale, not getting any sleep, but it's never dull and you can joke about it afterwards.

One night I was working with Tommy Hunt loading out and we were one down in the count, one beast short. Now Tommy is not a calm man under stress and when the pressure's really on he tends to flap his arms a bit.

So he's wandering up and down the catwalk, flapping his arms about and the driver who we call 'Bullet' (and not 'cause he's quick) is supposed to be helping him.

Well Bullet got tired of all the fuss and lay down on the catwalk for a little rest. Meanwhile Tommy's up and down, flapping his arms, stepping over the snoozing driver four or five times, trying to do his job and put things right.

This went on for 20 minutes till Bullet surfaced and remarked: "So you right now Tom?"

One of the horsemen bringing cattle up to the loading area wore a big black hat, had a big American saddle and rode a piebald horse. We called him 'Tonto'.

Anyway, he's coming up the lane when a renegade steer escaped through the loading gate and took off across the flat.

Tonto to the rescue!

He hits the ramp at half a gallop and spurs the piebald to take off like the Man from Snowy River, but horse props, Tonto is catapulted into space and lands with a sickening thud on very hard bitumen.

We all just stood there with mouths open till old mate recovered sufficiently to stand up and you could see he wasn't badly hurt, then we all burst out laughing. It was really very funny!

Bruce Riehl is based in Toowoomba with Robertson's Transport; he's been coming out to Roma for 10 years.

"I head out early on a Tuesday morning with whatever's left in the yard - a double or a B-double or a road train. Wouldn't miss it; it's the main event of the week, a day in paradise … and I would have worn me best cap had I known you were going to take me photo!"

Neil McIntosh, Lightning Ridge NSW, gets up to Roma several times a year. The day I first met him he had some of his own cattle together with those of his neighbours making up a full load for his AB-triple.

"What did you think of the sale?"

"The trucks are our main business but we do have a few cattle. You saw those black steers we sold today at 210c/kg? Well a couple of months ago I passed them in at Walgett a 130c/kg. You could say I'm more than pleased with the result and I'm glad I came to Roma!"

David Scott always wanted to have trucks!

He grew up on the family property "Crochdantigh" Muckadilla where his parents encouraged him to learn to drive at an early age.

In 1982 when he was barely old enough to shave and certainly too young to apply for a licence, he took his first load to Roma – Crochdantigh cattle in the station body truck.

"I was in awe of the place," he recalls. "To be in there, fully loaded in our F7 Ford alongside all the truckies in their double deckers and road trains was very exciting for me.

Tommy Grace was there; he wouldn't have been much older than me. He must have read my mind because he came over a said:

'Don't worry, son; plenty more years left in you yet!'

From then on I planned to have my own trucking company and in 1998 my wife Margot and I started Scotts Haulage. We've had our ups and downs but we're still here, still having fun, and have built the business to the stage that we now operate six trucks."

Well that was the story we put to bed and it would have stayed just like that but two weeks after those lines were typed, David was hurt.

He was loading bullocks up the crush when one rushed back on him, jammed him against the gate and smashed his pelvis. He was in hospital for seven weeks and when he came out he spent another two weeks in a wheelchair. During that time, Margot ran the show.

David was still convalescing when he told me:

"She's doing a great job and the figures are up; I think the customers prefer to deal with her rather than me."

All the Scotts are big men; Margot is just the opposite. She's a pretty little thing and you would see her around the yards in her blue and white Nike joggers, wearing a colourful shirt and three quarter jeans, going about her business with that stunning smile of hers as if she had been doing it all her life.

After one sale a Scotts Haulage truck was loading out when I spotted Margot in action. She was about 100 metres away, too far to take a photo and I didn't have a camera with me anyway, but the image is fixed permanently in my brain

Here was this tiny figure standing beside the truck, a big Century Class 120 Freightliner; she had a flapper in one hand and a mobile phone up to her ear in the other, and she was looking up into the open door of the cab talking to the driver and relaying instructions.

My mind flashed back to the diminutive Chinese student who stopped a tank Tiananmen Square. The Power of One!

Good on you, Margot!

4. Vendors

They come from all over Australia, literally!

While a high percentage of the cattle come from local or near local areas, many travel huge distances to get here and for good reason: it's the biggest cattle selling centre in Australia with the most consistent market ... and it's on every week!

It has been said, *"The only time there is no store sale in Roma on a Tuesday is when the Tuesday falls on Good Friday!"*

Frank Booth "Cowie" Cloncurry not only sends cattle down to Roma but most times he comes down with them.

We've been comin' here for over 20 years. First we went to Winton and Emerald but once we tried Roma we stuck to it.

Mostly I come down with the cattle, come down as a passenger in one of the trucks, otherwise I come down in me Toyota and bring me bikes down to either get 'em serviced or trade 'em in on new ones.

I get the vehicle serviced at Mohr's Garage, the best in town, and buy clothes at Golders for meself and the wife. They all laugh when I shop for me wife but that doesn't worry me a bit.

I used to stay at the Aussie Battler motel but over the latter few years the Ayers family, George and his wife Shirl, have confiscated me and taken me to their farm and knocked a bit of work out of me.

Teal is the daughter and then the young bloke Coben who I call Joe; very happy family and they all look after me very well.

Besides selling down here I've also bought cattle. I've picked up a couple of pens of classy Walker heifers from "Tara" and also some of Paul Robinson's older breeders in store condition from "Waverley" at Augathella.

Those Robinson cows turned out beautiful and I'm still breedin' out of them; wouldn't mind a few more.

I've also managed to get hold of some good bulls at the right price, bulls going to slaughter – Alastair Bassingthwaighte's Santa bulls and Charolais bulls bred by Boyd Harms.

Roma is like a second home to me. They tell me I must have a home here or a girlfriend, but you can cut out that girlfriend business; there's nothin' like that goin' on!

Bob Hall "Greenmulla" Quilpie first came to a saleyards in Roma in 1955 on his way back from the Brisbane Exhibition with his grandfather William Alexander Hall.

The Hall family connection with the Quilpie district dates back to the 1890s; Bob is a fourth generation Bulloo River grazier and, with grandsons on the ground it won't be long before it's six generations.

All the store cattle he produces are sold at Roma and, when seasons are right and there is surplus feed, he buys here as well.

Roma is the only place we buy in the saleyards, mainly because of the selection available and the breed types on offer. We know if we come here we can find cattle that are suited to our country.

You come here, they're all penned up, they're well presented, the names are on the gates, you know where they come from, and by selecting cattle from similar country to our own we know they are going to do well for us.

People think of Roma as being a long way from Quilpie. That certainly would have been the case for Pasty Durack when he came here from Thylungra in 1869; but things are a bit different these days.

We find it very handy. We're only five hours away on an excellent road, we have our own truck, we can have cattle in a holding paddock one day, in Roma Saleyards and sold the next, shrinkage is minimal, we get an excellent price, and we'll keep comin' back.

At the moment we have a great season, the best since 1971. We are checking out the market today but we'll be back to buy next week and we'll keep coming back till we fill our country up again.

Bevan & Allison Doyle "Tumbar" Jericho have been sending cattle to Roma for three years. This is the story they told on 27th March 2007, the day their No.6 steers were sold:

We were into breeding softer cattle and custom feeding them for Woolworths but when the feedlot we were using changed hands and the new owners discontinued the arrangements, we looked at different ways to market our cattle.

Roma is the benchmark of the industry. You talk to people and they'll all say, "Oh but at Roma ..." and they'll quote you what's happening there.

So we came to Roma.

In 2004 we sent in 36 decks of our steers, 1432 head all No.3s, and were we delighted with the resultant $574 average. We reckoned we made the right decision.

We have been back every year since then. Feedlotters and backgrounders have come to know our cattle and how they perform and we are seeing repeat buyers back here year after year which is encouraging us to continue with our composite breeding programme and to produce what the market wants.

We come here because we feel we are getting a premium on the day and we get to expose our cattle to the wider community; even those who don't buy our cattle get to see our cattle and they might decide to have a bid on them next time.

It's a great exercise for us too. Really it's only just down the road , we come down to see the cattle sold, we get to meet the people, we see the same faces, we talk to the buyers, we talk to the agents; it's a business day but it's also a day out.

Michael Barron bought for the AACo today; they know the cattle, they've had 'em before and they are consistent purchasers.

So too Elders Meandarra, Terry Lanskey, and you see he had young Glen Waldron doing the job so you can imagine the contact with their Meandarra clients will continue when Terry retires.

We've just said g'day to Alan Bignell. We've known Alan for 20 years. He bought 194 of our steers today and it's to be hoped he does well out of them and comes back for more next year.

We enjoy the cafeteria, the food is excellent, we like watching the cattle being weighed and then we have a steak sandwich! Sometimes we even come out for breakfast and catch up with people before the sale starts. It's a day when we can mingle with people in the business.

Roma Saleyards is a focal point of the cattle industry in Queensland and it's good for us to come here and meet them every so often; you see people here that you don't see anywhere else.

As everyone knows, Jericho is on the Jordan River; and Tumbar is too. In the last 36 months we have sold 5131 steers here, steers that have drunk the holy waters of the River Jordan and grazed on the buffel pastures that we established in 1962, and they have averaged over $600.

So we'll be back! But now it's time to go home and finish branding the No.7s and get them ready for next year. See ya then!

Trevor & Jenny York "Hyde Park" Wallumbilla breed top quality Simmental cattle. They spoke to me after selling four pens of 400kg plus feeder steers to a NSW feedlot at very good money:

We have sold here a lot and we've never had a bad sale here.

The market can fluctuate, but comparing our cattle and prices with other cattle and their prices, we're satisfied that we've received value on the day and that's why we say we've never had a bad sale.

Apart from that we both like coming here. You rub shoulders with other people in the industry and you get to see different cattle.

"I'm surprised at the number of women that don't come," said Jenny. "The husbands come but the women drop them off and go."

"I think it's important to see your cattle sold, to meet the buyers, to understand what's going on. I've met a lot of buyers; I know them and they know me. I think it all helps."

We met a new buyer today; Andrew Talbot from Elders in Tamworth buying for Killara feedlot at Quirindi.

He bought the four pens and when they've been fed for 100 days, he's is going to send us photos and details of how they hang up. You can't build an association like that unless you're here.

It's also good to be able to go up to a buyer and thank him for his support; he appreciates it too. Most people think of buyers only as people who are trying to rip you off, but we're all in this business together, one can't survive without the other, and we should be working together to produce a better article.

And the canteen! You've gotta have a cuppa tea, you've gotta have a steak sandwich. If you don't have a steak sandwich you're missing out on the best steak sandwich in Queensland.

You can sit down, relax, have a yarn; it's a great place to learn what's going on. We never miss calling in before we go home.

A few years back, when Cath Cocks was still there, Jenny and I walked up to the counter and Cath said:

"It's good to see a husband and wife who talk to each other."

"How do you know we were talking and not arguing?"

"Because Jenny was smiling."

"She was smiling because she won the argument!"

Would be nice to think we'll see the "Hyde Park" cattle and Jenny's smile around Roma Saleyards for a long time yet!

Les Latemore "The Lamen" Roma is getting on in years and it's hard to have a conversation with him because he's practically deaf.

He's been selling through Roma Saleyards for as long as he or anyone else can remember and he likes to top the sale, not necessarily in terms of cents per kilo but definitely in dollars per head, so he breeds Charolais cross bullocks, really big buggers.

He is a dry old codger with a great sense of humour. Talking about ageing, he said to me one day:

"At one time you'd stumble and fall and put out your hands – now the first thing that hits the ground is your head."

Bobby & Mary Quinlan "Yanna" Charleville have been sending cattle to Roma since 1979 and haven't missed a year since then with consignments of fats as well as stores:

"This is the place to be," they say. "In 2000 we got 234c/kg for Charbray weaner steers – fairy tale stuff! Where else would you get a deal like that?

No wonder it's the biggest cattle selling centre in Australia!"

David Hardie "Dumfries" Blackall is a regular supporter:

"When we lived at Jandowae, I'd come to Roma to buy cattle; I'd either buy them myself or get Terry Ryan to do the job for me.

Then we moved out to Blackall and now I sell cattle at Roma; sometimes I come down myself to see them sold.

Roma is a great place to buy cattle or sell cattle and on top of that you are always guaranteed of a good feed at the canteen and the opportunity to see a few friendly faces and have a yarn."

Rick & Bob Summerville "Glenbrook" Charleville are twin brothers and two of the nicest gentlemen you could ever wish to meet; Rick is pleased to tell you he is the elder by eight minutes.

They operate as Summerville Pastoral Co in partnership with Bob's wife, Jeanette, and have been selling cattle here for 20 years.

"We mostly sell our boner cows and old bulls but sometimes a few cows & calves and our weaners," they told me during a fat sale.

"We enjoy coming here; it's a day out for us. We've always been satisfied with the prices, we get a bit of attention from the agents, we like the canteen, in fact we had breakfast there this morning.

And we'll be back."

Alick Osborne is the manager of "Gwambegwine" at Taroom where Daandine Pastoral Co. breeds top quality Santa Gertrudis cattle. He had a consignment of 327 steers at Roma in May 2007 and he was there with the Managing Director, Jan Clark, co-director John Robbins and the agent Tony Pearce.

Over a cup of tea they talked about Roma Saleyards:

"We've been coming here for 20 years," said Alick. "We sell steers here every year but we've also sold cows, cows & calves and heifers."

"We use Roma quite a bit," Jan commented. "In the Clark & Tait group, we often send cattle here from Enniskillen at Tambo and there'll be another lot of them next week.

I enjoy it here; it's a good centre. I've been here many times to see the Gwambegwine cattle sold. Alick used to send them in to the special Santa Gertrudis sales and sometimes we'd win the prize for the best pen of feeder steers and if we didn't win we'd run second."

"Where else would you go?" asked John Robbins. "As a director I have a marketing responsibility and it's up to me to recommend the best outlet for whatever cattle they have to sell.

You take Roma! It's pretty handy; it attracts big numbers of cattle and all the buyers. The Gwambegwine cattle have established a reputation here over the years, everyone knows 'em, and they always sell very well."

Tony Pearce chimed in: "He's right! Year in year out, this is a great place to sell cattle; takes a lot of beating! There is no doubt that this is the place to sell the Gwambegwine cattle."

"We've had some exciting times here," said John. "Remember last year when Wallace Logan bought the lot, 224 of them, and they averaged $1011 a head. We'd be mad not to come back!"

"This year was exciting too," said Alick. "I got thrown off a horse the day before we had 'em in the yards and I could only use one arm. Tony turned up to help but he had a crook back. We were both pretty useless in the yards but thankfully we have good staff and the drafting and trucking went ahead on time."

"We've also bought here," said Jan. "John and I came here last October to buy bulls. We particularly wanted a red Brahman bull to use in our stud and we finished up paying the top price on the day.

They presented me with a bottle of rum which was very handy at that time of the year; it finished up in the Christmas pudding!"

Gary & Kerry Ladbrook "Bulah" Yuleba breed good quality crossbred cattle and sell both fats and stores at Roma.

They sold heavy, milk tooth, feeder steers in the store sale last week at 195c/kg and had two decks of bullocks in the fat sale the day I caught up with Gary:

"Our place is between Yuleba and Wandoan," he says, "so we are a lot closer to Wandoan than Roma, however, we decided to come to Roma when Wandoan sale dates became irregular. Roma had better competition and was on every week.

I normally come down to see the cattle sold, have a bit of a yarn and talk to the agent. Roma is a good setup and I would like to think it will stay that way."

Will Abel Smith, a Director and Livestock Manager of S. Kidman & Co Ltd based in Adelaide, is responsible for the sales programme of all Kidman cattle.

During the drought years since the turn of the century, 75,000 Kidman cattle from their various Channel Country properties as well as Quinyambie in South Australia have been sold through Roma.

"We have marketed all types of stores through the saleyards and now that our country has received good rain we are using Roma to buy cattle to restock. We've bought 8,000 so far this year.

"Roma to me has always been the place to go," says Will.

Ian Murray, Kindee Pastoral Co., has been selling his weaners in Roma for 20 years. They come in from "Cowangah" at Taroom and "Muya" at Injune, all on the one day, and when I spoke to him in June 2007 he had just sold 854 steers with the heifer draft to follow.

"We consider we've got good quality cattle and anyone who has bought them before has come back for more. Today again the bulk of the cattle were purchased by repeat buyers.

This is what sticks to us, our reputation, so that in spite of the drought there has been very good competition today and we are very happy with the prices.

In 2005 our weaner steers averaged 266c/kg for 273kg and $729 which they tell me is a record. This year they've sold to 217c/kg and averaged 202.5c/kg for 290kg which is $596 a head, in a drought!

We've got to be happy with that; that's why we come here … and we'll be back next year!

Rob & Alex Taylor run a lot of cattle at "Kevington" and "South Westgrove" at Injune. I caught up with them after a fat sale and asked them why they choose to sell at Roma.

"Well I started selling here when I first came to the district in 1978 and I've found this the best place to market my store cattle.

We had Herefords and we were selling a lot of steers, heavy feeder steers, lighter steers and PTIC heifers. We found the Stuarts Creek sales in March and the Special Hereford sales in July to be the ideal outlets for all our sale cattle."

"I like to come in with Robert to see our cattle sold," says Alex. "The very first time was an eye-opener.

It was just after we were married. We came in through the gate, walked down the lane, poked our noses over the fence and, oops! … here are some of our cattle that had no business being there.

The Stock Squad was called, that put a scatter in the camp and created quite a bit of interest for the day, but we ended up with the proceeds so we came out of that one alright."

Rob takes up the story: "Apart from anything else it's a great meeting place especially after those big special sales we used to have.

We'd all be here at the sale, then we'd have a bit of a party down town at the Queens Arms, then we'd move on to the Maranoa Club and we'd end up in John "Jack" Mulcahy's motel room with a bottle of rum in the early hours of the morning."

"Alex, how did you get him home?" I asked.

"With great difficulty!" she replied.

"These days Roma is the major selling centre; there will always be a Roma Saleyards," says Rob.

"It attracts people and cattle from all over Australia, which is fantastic for the industry really, and we'll keep on coming here."

Bill Hartley has been around Roma all his life.

Fifty years ago he had "Sunnyvale" down Hartley's Lane just north of town. Today, Bill and his sons Bill, Tom and John, operate as a family partnership and they have seven places from Injune to Aramac and run about 16,000 cattle.

Bill is often referred to as "Grandad" and I guess that helps to distinguish him from his son, Bill, but before we spoke about the saleyards I asked him about the name.

The first bloke to call me Grandad was a chap named Brother Edwards who used to work for me.

He was a helluva good worker and time meant nothing to him. If you wanted him early, he'd arrive out there at two or three o'clock in the morning, and he'd work all day and never complain about knocking off late. He was a really good worker.

Anyhow, he gave me the name even before any grandkids arrived … well, I might have had one or two … but it was Brother Edwards that called me Grandad before anyone else.

He was a character and he'd get up to all sorts of tricks.

Joey Higgins had a mare and foal running on the common. It was a big lump of a filly foal and Brother took a fancy to it.

As soon as it was big enough, Brother caught it and broke it in and he was riding it one day when Joey came up to him in a car and asked had he seen his missing filly.

Brother said he remembered the foal but hadn't seen it for a while; he suggested that Joey jump on his horse and have a good look around and see if he could find it.

So Joey rode off on the filly he was looking for, didn't find her, and then handed her back.

Brother thought that was very funny!

The conversation came back to the saleyards and Bill continued:

We have sold a lot of cattle here over the years, we buy bulls here, and we have a fair idea of what goes on here.

We prefer to sell our cattle as fats unless the season dictates otherwise. In the past we have used Toowoomba a lot but in the last 12 to 18 months Roma has been a better market so we come here.

Thinking back, I would say that John Molony was the best Stud Stock auctioneer in his day and undoubtedly Garth Hughes is the number one man today. He has a wonderful memory for the buyers' names and property names too; I'm sure he impresses a lot of people.

Blake Munro was one of the best Fat Stock auctioneers, one of the best all round auctioneers. He never punted cattle along, there was no bullshit about him, and he was right on the value of the cattle on the day; in lots of ways he was very much like Leo McMahon.

Among the buyers, Wallace Logan impressed me. If he wanted 'em he bought 'em, two or three pens at a time … or the whole lane.

And as far as presenting your cattle, Georgie Ayers does a great job the way he drafts the different lines. I have heard it said that no one has ever whinged about the way George has drafted their cattle. I think that says a lot for his ability.

The saleyards, well it's like a big drama that keeps unfolding:

There are ups and downs, cold days and wet days, market fluctuations, and there seems to be no end to laws that must be complied with, but Roma has kept going and established itself as a big selling centre, the major selling centre, and it probably will remain so.

I'm just pleased to have seen it develop as much as it has over the last 50 years.

John Galwey was a young agent with Australian Estates when he came to Roma on a two-week relieving stint in 1964. He's still here!

John says he was lucky to work for two great agents: Dave Watkins in Rockhampton and Ardie Slaughter in Roma, and both of them had a lasting influence on him.

But he didn't stay an agent for long. In 1965 Ken Tomkins offered him a position at "Stuarts Creek", the home of the famous Stuarts Creek Hereford Stud, and he left the agency to branch into a different division of the pastoral industry.

By the mid seventies, he was well established at Stuarts Creek, he was a Bungil Shire councillor, a member of the Saleyards Board and his flew his own plane. This is his story:

Liveweight selling of fat cattle was becoming accepted, Cannon Hill saleyards in Brisbane had adopted the practice in 1976 and the Roma Saleyards Board was thinking of following suit.

I was very keen for this to happen, so too was my good mate Barrie Loughnan who was also on the Board, but we weren't getting anywhere, we were becoming frustrated, so we decided to fly down and have a look at established liveweight scales in NSW.

It was Barrie's first flight in a light aircraft. As we taxied onto the Stuarts Creek strip he wanted to smoke; I wouldn't let him, but he had one going by the time we were two inches off the ground.

We spent three days away, went to Tamworth, Quirindi and Dubbo, inspected their facilities, came back and drew up plans for Roma, presented these to the Board, the powers-that-be got upset they hadn't been invited, so we did the trip all over again.

Well that got things moving and in 1978 Roma became a liveweight selling centre, the second in Queensland after Cannon Hill and about the same time as Dalby.

We had always supported the yards with both fat and store cattle at the regular sales but, over a few beers with Des Cherry one night, we came up with the idea of a special sale, a Special Hereford Store Sale to promote Hereford cattle and Stuarts Creek bulls.

The plan was that only Stuarts Creek bull-buying clients would be invited to sell in the sale, for that I was a bit unpopular, but in 1985 the first Stuarts Creek Hereford Sale attracted a yarding of 6,500 stores, buyers came from the three eastern states and paid a premium.

It was a highly successful event.

The second year, we yarded 7,000. Wallace Logan turned up, bought two lanes of cattle from three vendors in three bids, blew all existing records out of the sky, and went home with about 800 head.

The cattle he took belonged to John & Jill Frith "Wondolin" Roma, the next lot were our own Stuarts Creek cattle, and the third lot belonged to Charlie & Elizabeth Frith "Glen Arden" Roma.

The next year he came back and did the same.

By the late eighties the annual Stuarts Creek sale in March was the most talked about store sale in the country. Everybody wanted to be in it and new clients bought our bulls to secure an invitation.

It was good for Herefords, it was good for Stuarts Creek, it was good for Roma and it was good for Roma Saleyards … and on the social side, these big sales created a wonderful party atmosphere.

We'd all go to the QA after the sale, everyone would be happy, the grog flowed, the jokes followed, it was a great time to be alive.

There'd be 20 or 30 of us including Robbie Taylor, Tom Sloan the American, and I remember Jack Mulcahy at the bar with a glazed look in his eye and he came out with,

"You can't beat this, it's better than any holiday."

"What do you mean, Jack?"

"You bring your cattle in, sell 'em, have a few beers with your mates, skite and tell lies; this'll do me for a good day out."

The concept of a special breed sale had taken off with a bang and other special sales followed.

Within a few years the Hereford Society had established an annual Hereford sale in July, then there were series of special Santa Gertrudis sales and a couple of Charolais and Charolais cross sales.

In the early days, you could be assured of a premium at any of these special sales but after a time they lost their gloss a bit, however, during the nineties they certainly contributed to putting Roma on the map as the major selling centre in Australia.

These days I've heard Brendan Wade claim that Roma has a special store sale every Tuesday. When you think about it, that's true!

I'm a great advocate of the auction system and a supporter of Roma Saleyards. As I look back over the years I'm pleased that I played a role in establishing liveweight selling here.

Mind you, when we were weighing 500 fats a week, I never imagined we'd be weighing 10,000 to 12,000 stores, but that's what's happened and it's become a much bigger centre than I ever envisaged.

I only hope it continues to develop and that in another 20 or 30 years it will still be the leading cattle selling centre in Australia.

Ian & Joy Macallister had just sold 123 Angus cross weaner steers from "Roma Downs" when I caught up with Ian and asked him about his association with Roma Saleyards.

I first came to Roma as a cadet with Australian Estates in the mid fifties; Ardie Slaughter was the manager and Don Henning was the auctioneer. There were three sets of yards here in those days

Garth Hughes and I had started as message boys with Estates in the old Creek Street office in Brisbane. All he wanted to do was get into Stud Stock; all I wanted to do was go bush and learn to be a stock and station agent. I got my chance with the move to Roma.

Fifty years later we own quite a bit of country around here and we sell a lot of cattle through the saleyards. It's the biggest selling centre in Australia and, in my opinion, the best organised.

Our cattle vary a bit through the calving period but by coming here they can be drafted up into lines instead of having mixed lots in the paddock. I'm sure we get far better competition that way.

There are some people who are prepared to dump buckets on this place; they want to invent a new system.

But I say, if it ain't broke don't fix it, just keep improving it.

That's what's happening here now and has been happening for the last 15 years. Every time you come here there is more work going on and I reckon the Board is on the right track.

Roma is getting better all the time and we'll keep selling here.

5. Workers

If you go out to the saleyards on sale day, marvel at the auctioneers in action and watch the cattle being weighed, you could think you've seen all there is to see and that you understand how it works.

Believe me there is a lot more to it than that.

A band of workers behind the scenes keeps the whole place functional and when you read this chapter you'll understand that there would be no sale in Roma without them.

Keith Kimlin OAM was the Superintendent at the saleyards from January 1975 until his "Independence Day", 4th July 1996, when he retired. For those 21½ years he was on the job, day and night, living at the yards in the house provided by the Board.

During that time there were a heap of changes at the yards: the liveweight selling of fats was introduced and scales installed; steel yards gradually replaced the timber yards; liveweight selling of stores began; the curfew changed from dry to wet; water was made available to every pen; and the throughput of cattle escalated.

With the advent of political correctness Keith's title changed to "Foreperson in Charge", the most ridiculous name ever conceived, but it didn't alter his role which was to be responsible for the day to day management of the saleyards and all the duties that went with it.

Prior to starting at the saleyards, Keith had 22 years in the Police Force including time with the Stock Squad. Some said this background was well suited to the new portfolio!

In later years, when asked if his experiences confirmed what Stock Squad officers always suspected of the cattle duffing activities of certain individuals, he would reply in one word: "Yes!"

But enough of that; let's hear what Keith has to say these days:

Many of the little incidents had to do with truckies:

One night just after I started, a truckie backed up to the ramp to unload. He was having difficulty squaring up to the ramp and Roy Harms was there trying to give directions but was doing no good.

Anyway, this truckie got out of his truck, came up to Roy and swung a punch at his head. Roy ducked, Charlie Cosgrove came on the scene to help him and no real harm was done.

The driver must have been on pills or something!

A truckie from NSW pulled up at the ramp. I was up on the catwalk and he staggered over towards me and he said,

"Can you tell me where I am?"

"You are at the Roma Saleyards."

"Thank God for that; this is where I'm supposed to be."

He was full of yippee beans and he wanted to load cattle out. I refused. I told him we wouldn't load him for at least another four or five hours and that the best thing he could do was park his truck and have a sleep.

It was just before 2.00am when the phone rang and one of the agents told me about a cow stuck in the grid, the one on the highway, and because she was there no one could drive into or out of the saleyards.

I got the rifle, the bobcat and a couple of chains and went down to have a look thinking I would have to shoot her and pull her out, but when I got there I realised she hadn't broken a leg or anything and that she was worth saving if we could.

So we put a chain around her horns and around the bucket of the bobcat, and I slowly lifted her straight up in the air, right up high trying to get her back legs clear of the grid.

You can just imagine the scene in the middle of the night. There were blokes all round, car lights for illumination, trucks banked up waiting to get in and out, the cow suspended perpendicular in mid air … and along come a fully loaded tour bus and pulls up for a look.

So I swung the bobcat around, put the cow on the ground, undone the chain, hoped like hell it would fall off, which it did, and I hightailed it out of there on the bobcat and went back to bed.

A semi took off one night; he must've forgot to shut the back door and bloody cattle went everywhere, all over the highway, right down as far as the Surat turnoff, and the truck kept going towards Wallumbilla.

We rang the police, they chased the truck, there were no horsemen handy, so we rounded of the cattle up using cars, bloody agents cars – they're used to that.

Anyway it was a hairy ride but as luck would have it we got 'em, got 'em all, and we poked 'em back through the gate into the little paddock in front of the canteen.

The coppers pulled the truck up at Blythedale.

Another night there was this cow that jumped out of a double decker. She had a broken leg, was on the highway, in the middle of the road, and the police were there.

And I said to this copper, I said, "Shoot the bastard and let's get her out of here."

But he said, "Oh no, no, no, no; I'm not allowed to."

And I said, "Give us your gun," and I got it and went BOOM! ... and that was the end of that.

You've gotta do these things; I wanted to get back to bed!

A horse bit me once.

There was this big brown blood stallion on its way to Quilpie and he was spelling here at the yards.

Doug Wilson was looking after it and he had it in one of those yards up behind the paint shed, a big yard with a bit of shade in it, and was feeding it hay for a couple of days.

I was going past and I noticed that he had a front leg up over the top rail and up against the post and he couldn't get it off. I knew that if he was left there he would do serious damage.

I got in under him, lifted the hoof up and got him out of trouble but the ungrateful big brown bastard bit me; he latched on to my gut and hung on and just wouldn't let go.

I tell you what, it was bloody painful, and even though I poked his eyes and did everything he hung on and hung on. I was in agony.

Eventually he did let go and I finished up with the biggest love bite ever seen in Roma; without a word of a lie the swollen bruise was the size of a football and I still have a lump there to remind me of it.

They gave me a tetanus needle for the bite and the doctor diagnosed the lump as a possible hernia but the local vet, Ross Teitzel, said it was contused fat.

Anyhow, Workers Compensation was involved so I had to fly to Brisbane for a second opinion.

Dr Leaming, who used to be the Flying Surgeon at Longreach, took one look at it and said,

"Well lad, if that thing ever turns into a bloody hernia and comes against you in later life, I'll take it out for nothing."

I was very relieved and went and had a few beers before catching the plane back to Roma.

And then of course there were the agents:

One night we were locking off the troughs. The dry curfew was still on and all troughs had to be covered and locked at 8.00pm.

Des Collinson was doing the job and I was giving him a hand when along came one of the agents most upset; he was mouthing off, cursing all and sundry, and started abusing Des.

Well Des took it for a while but in the end it got too much so he walked over to the agent and said,

"What you need is a good kick up the arse; shut ya mouth!"

The agent, who was a much smaller man, told him something rude, which I won't repeat here, and that really put Des's hackles up and he made a grab for him.

But the little bloke was too quick; he slipped through the rails and took off and Des couldn't catch him so he came back and we continued to lock off the troughs.

I'll never forget one morning before a store sale. It was fairly early, perhaps about 7 o'clock, and an agent came to me and said,

"I'm in strife."

"Who did you murder?"

"Nobody, but I've got six decks of cattle here from Cloncurry and no paperwork whatsoever. I won't be able to sell 'em. We'll either have to hold them over to next week or send them on to Dalby."

I said, "You won't be sending them to Dalby that's for sure. Give me the name of your vendor and any other details you have then you disappear for a while. Leave this with me"

I reckoned it was no good beating about the bush so I asked the Stock Inspector to come into my office and told him the story. No problem. He got on the phone and rang his counterpart in Cloncurry.

The bloke up there knew the owner, knew the cattle, knew about the load, and he volunteered to fax us a duplicate set of papers straight away.

By 9 o'clock we had everything sorted out much to the relief of the agent concerned and I said to him,

"There's always a way around a problem, legitimately, if you are open and honest about it. In this case the authorities were only too pleased to co-operate once they realised we were on the level."

It was during the Beef Depression and a drought that this pen of 15 or 20 head of poor cattle was passed in; there was just no bid.

The agent came to me the day after the sale to request that I unlock the gate so that he could remove the stock from the saleyards.

When I did that, he let them out onto the stock route, got in his car and drove away saying,

"I never want to see the bastards again!"

Another agent came to me one day to borrow a pocket knife.

I had a very good knife, a Boker, and I was always reluctant to lend it, but he wanted to cut the twine off a bale of hay and you try to get on with everybody as best you can, so I lent it to him.

"Bring it straight back," I told him.

He brought it back in two pieces! I wasn't impressed. After that day I never carried a pocket knife to the yards again.

That particular agent was transferred up north and I was pleased to see him go.

You try to make yourself available to agents and buyers and the general public and I think I got on well with most of them; in fact I made many good friends over the years.

Sandy Kidd from Windorah always struck me as a terribly decent fella; Wallace Logan used to ring me from Normanton to check on the market; and I had a lot of time for Peter Knauer.

Peter "The Feather" Knauer bought a lot of cattle in those days, thousands of them. This day he wasn't there and they held up the sale for him.

It was 11.05am, the auction should have started at 11.00am sharp and I asked them what was going on.

"Waiting for Knauer," they said.

With that The Feather came along and I said to him,

"They waited for you to start the sale."

"Never do that," he said. "Never wait for me; if I want cattle I'll be here in plenty of time. As it is I'm not buying at all today."

Certain names have been withheld to either (a) protect the innocence of the living or (b) in reverence to the memory of the dead.

Doug Wilson was a stockman at the yards from 1980. Prior to that he had managed places for the AP Company - "Womblebank" north of Mitchell and "Robinson River" up in The Gulf - so he knew men, he knew stock and he had a wealth of experience.

I knew Doug, I worked with him, but Mick Connell worked with him longer and knew him better so I'll let him tell the story:

Doug Wilson was our man, the Elders stockman, at the saleyards and he did everything for us. With Johnny Martyn he did the drafting, he did all our feeding, and he also did all the odd jobs like unloading trucks and tending to sick cattle.

He was very loyal, was not afraid of hard work, hours meant nothing to him, he had a dry sense of humour, and he taught me a lot about people and about exotic cattle.

I came up from Victoria about the same time Doug arrived and I remember him asking me to look out for dogbites as we drafted these cattle from The North.

Well I was looking around the hocks and the shins but he said,

"No, you stupid bastard, up here, up around the hindquarters and the loins," and then he explained how dingoes attack the young calves and the lucky ones survive but are dogbitten.

The wounds heal but leave deep scars that detract from the sale value of the adult animal and it's best to draft them out from the main line and sell them separately.

You can't learn that in Victoria; you've gotta come to Roma!

Another time he saved me from going to jail.

It was about 1.00am in the morning. I was out at the yards, hot and sweaty in a pair of shorts and an old singlet, covered in shit, but I had to duck back into town for a permit at the office.

I raced in, opened up the office, grabbed the paperwork, and took off again in a hurry back to the yards.

There had been a spate of break-and-enters in town at the time and the security forces were on high alert. One of the officers must have seen me taking off in a hurry and he followed.

As soon as I pulled up he was out of his car, accused me of robbing Elders, and asked me to accompany him to the police station.

I had no identification with me; to him I suppose I looked a bit iffy, anyway, there was no way he was going to believe my story until Doug turned up.

"She's right mate; he's with me, he's a bloody agent." And old mate was satisfied so we got back to work.

Doug would take six weeks holiday a year and go to Burleigh Heads. He loved it and he thrived on it.

He would put on a lot of weight and come back three stone heavier but he would lose it all again within three weeks.

Apart from all the good work he did for Elders he helped plenty of others and he also did jobs for the Board.

What sort of jobs? The shit jobs no one else wanted to do!

He cleaned out the water troughs, cared for the forgotten cattle that others had left behind, and once in a while he would paint all the timber rails with a mixture of linseed oil and turps to preserve the timber and stop it from cracking.

Then Doug got sick, very sick; they found he had cancer in the jaw and an operation was necessary.

It was a massive procedure that lasted 20 hours but Doug survived and came back to work with very visible scars and a different way of speaking, but there was no change to his attitude to the job or the hours he put in.

Eventually, his health deteriorated to the extent that he had to give it away and he and his wife, Lorna, retired to Toowoomba where Doug died at home in his lounge chair in May 1995.

That was the way he wanted to go.

We still miss him and those that knew him still talk about him. He was one of the best!

I don't know about you, but I have never seen a memorial service for anybody at any saleyards, but when Doug died such a service was held for him on the lawn outside the canteen.

I believe it was organised by Cath Cocks, Mick Connell and Blake Munro and you can bet Keith Kimlin had something to do with it as well. Anyway they did a great job; it was something special.

The ceremony was conducted by Father Michael Cooney, a big man who looked even bigger in his vestments, and it was held just before the start of the store sale so there were a lot of people present.

"It was a fitting tribute to a fella who had put in so much at the yards. Doug was a very experienced stockman who would do anything to assist anybody," said Keith Kimlin. "It was very moving to see all those bare heads bowed in his honour."

Amanda Golden, the daughter of Hal & Mary Golden "Sollow" Yuleba, has worked at the yards for a few years, pushing cattle up over the scales, pencilling for the Board, and is now back at the scales.

She tells the story of an altercation with a blind heifer as being the highlight of her saleyard experiences so far:

It was sold as a single beast, poor thing, and it was blind so it couldn't see where to go. It was one pen back from the old scales, drafted off on its own, heading in the wrong direction and bumping into the rails.

I was trying to bring her onto the scales, she was heading the wrong way and I was trying to turn her back. I stepped in front of her and made a bit of a noise but she must have been deaf as well because she kept coming, trod on my foot, I went down and she walked all over the top of me. It didn't hurt much and I got up and kept going.

I love it here. I love the work, I love the cattle and I love the people I work with; it's great and I'll be here till my last breath!

Philip Edwards is the South East Queensland Supervisor for Livestock Link, the contract scanning company that reads all the NLIS eartags once the cattle are penned and before they are sold.

When those tags first became law, the Board installed Aleis lane readers at a cost of $270,000 but they were found to be unsatisfactory, too slow.

The technology worked, no doubt about that, but when a pen of 20 or 30 of cattle pushed and shoved their way off the scales and through the readers, they scanned 100% of the tags only 98% of the time, and that meant delays. The whole pen had to be redone till the beast that was missed was identified and scanned.

You know how it is in the supermarket. The customer turns up at the checkout with a trolley full of groceries and the operator checks them through reading the prices off the barcodes.

But the tomato sauce won't read it won't scan; no matter how many times the bottle is passed before the reader, you don't hear the little beep that tells you it's been accepted.

So there is a delay; either the supervisor comes along and sorts it out or they swap the bottle for one that does scan. Meantime the queue at the checkout grows longer.

That's okay at Woolies; at least they know from the outset which item is the holdup, but at the saleyards the non-reader still has to be found and the time wasted can be considerable, nerves fray, weighing time is extended, and it's just not good enough.

Enter Livestock Link. Since July 2006 their teams of five to nine people, using hand held Aleis scanners, have been reading every beast in the selling pens prior to the sales.

Philip Edwards explains the programme:

We do the Toowoomba sales early on Monday morning then come to Roma. At 9.00pm our people start scanning the stores and finish at about 5.00am Tuesday then go and have a sleep.

I get them up around midday to do any of the cows & calves that weren't penned in the first round and somewhere in between I manage to have a couple of hours camp myself.

Then we head off to Dalby.

The Dalby cattle are done on Tuesday night before the Wednesday sale, then it's back to Roma Wednesday evening to do the fats for Thursday, and we head to Goondiwindi after that if there is a sale there on the Friday.

At each venue, buyers can bid with confidence knowing that all cattle are in the system ready to be transferred to their new owners before the sale starts, and there is one little added advantage – we all know prior to the sale exactly how many cattle there are!

The good news is that (a) the system works very well and provides the traceability necessary to maintain our nation's reputation as the supplier of the best and cleanest beef in the world, and (b) the Board got $220,000 of its money back!

George & Shirley Ayers have been working at the saleyards with Elders since 1994, the year they were married. Blake Munro was the manager and Mick Connell had a hand in their appointment.

Since then they have drafted cattle, penned them up, booked them up and fed 'em. They have worked at all the regular sales plus bull sales and dispersal sales, and they were the first contractors to the Board to weigh and deliver the cattle when liveweight selling of stores was introduced.

I had a yarn to them when they were not too busy after a fat sale. The following story will give you an understanding of their roles, the hours they work and what they do to fill in their week:

On average, they handle 2000 cattle a week for Elders. George does all the drafting, Shirley helps with the penning and booking up, and they are both up on the catwalk with the auctioneer during the sale.

Apart from that they feed the cattle that come in early a day or two before the sale and any that need feeding after the sale.

George starts at about 6.00am on Monday feeding cattle while Shirley is in the office from 8.00am sorting out the bookings.

They go out to the yards after lunch and are there drafting and penning up anywhere from midnight till 2.00am depending on the numbers in the sale the next day

Tuesday starts at 6.30am and finishes when the work is done and usually that means some time after dark.

There is feeding and office work again on Wednesday morning getting ready for Thursday. In the afternoon the fats are drafted and once again the finishing time depends on numbers.

Shirley reckons there are always heaps of cattle on State of Origin night and they never get to see the game. One fella overcame that problem to a certain extent by bringing a radio that he perched up on a corner post at the draft so they could all at least listen.

From down the lane you could hear this bloke yelling out:

"What pen are you going to next and what's the score?"

The Thursday fat sale keeps them busy from early morning till the last of their cattle are weighed and then invariably there are cattle to be fed, and sometimes there is more feeding to be done on Friday.

Long distance cattle start coming in on Saturday and Sunday for the sale on Tuesday and they have to be fed as soon as they arrive which means they are feeding cattle every day of the week.

They go through 3000 round bales of hay a year which means they feed about 150,000 head annually.

On any given day there is work for them at the saleyards, but they also have two children; Teal is eight and Coben is 15 months so there is a young family to raise too.

Shirley does the cooking, except on Monday nights when they have hamburgers at the saleyards, and six years ago they bought a dishwasher that does the washing up.

But there is more! In cahoots with Dane Pearce, Shirley runs the NRL tipping competition for the Elders Roma branch and does a great job too. There is no cheating and the scores are always spot on!

You would reckon she'd be a fan of Friday Night Football?

"No, not me; too tired for that! Friday night is the one night of the week you'll find me in the cot very early," says Shirl.

I asked, "Do you enjoy this life?"

"It's good, really good," they replied in unison and you could tell by the happiness on their faces that they meant it. "You get used to it and you don't need many hours sleep."

"Tell me some of the things that happened, the funny things."

"Well," says George. "It wasn't funny at the time but you can look back on it now and have a laugh.

We had a fella working with us; Cecil Bland was his name. I was on the draft gate up the front and he was down the back of the pen standing beside the gate.

This big bullock came running through, Cecil just tapped him on the rump with his flapper and the bullock kicked out and caught him flush on the point of the jaw.

It was just like you see in a cartoon. He stood there swaying for a second then down he went, out cold. I thought he was actually dead! I've never seen anything like it.

I walked over to him … and he started snoring. That's when I knew he was alright.

We called the Ambulance.

Cecil was out for 10 or 15 minutes and we had to drag him out of the road to let the bullocks back, but the ambulance came, we got it up the lane, loaded Cecil aboard and away he went to hospital.

But he was okay the next day.

Another time we had a young agent named Ben Gleeson. He was in the pound huntin' 'em out when this old cow went in and she rolled Ben out of the pound past me.

Rolled him along like a ball and his notebook flew out into the middle of the yard and when he got up all he was worried about was losing his notebook, but he recovered that and we went on drafting."

Shirley took up the storytelling:

"We had this big AACo female dispersal on a Friday and started drafting cattle and mothering calves on the Tuesday afternoon.

We worked on Tuesday night, kicked back into 'em at 8 o'clock Wednesday morning, drafted all day and did the fats as well, started again Thursday during the fat sale, by Thursday night more than one bloke was cowboyin' it bad.

46

When you do this sort of work long enough, especially if you're not used to it, you get chaffed between the legs and in the cheeks of your bum, and the tendency is to spread your legs when you walk, just like cowboys do.

Anyway, Jason Carswell was suffering from the cowboy complaint more than most and he was seen in his stubby shorts, standing up on the platform behind the scalehouse, legs apart, wind blowing from the south, trying to get some relief.

He reckoned he was going to stay there for three hours or as long as the breeze kept up. It was hilarious!

When we were doing the contracting for the Board and putting cattle across the scales we had one bloke who couldn't hear and another bloke who couldn't count or read.

It took a couple of months to work 'em out but with the first bloke I learned to communicate in sign language and the second bloke we kept him right away from paperwork or counting and just got him to chase the cattle up the lane.

And it worked out very well for all concerned."

Finally I asked, "Where to from here?"

"This'll do us. We are part of the saleyards now; it's sort of been home for us for a fair while really, and we like the work, the people and the way of life. We'll be here till we get kicked out!"

Roma Saleyards wouldn't be the same without George and Shirley!

Des Collinson runs the scalehouse these days but he has done everything around the saleyards except be an agent and auctioneer.

Thirty years ago he was one of Keith Kimlin's men cleaning out the troughs, replacing broken rails, cleaning out the pens and whatever else had to be done to keep the job running smoothly.

Des worked the scales when they were first installed, he did the market reporting for a while, and on occasions he actually ran the place as the "Foreperson in Charge". But for the last ten years he's been in the scalehouse; a key figure in the whole operation.

Apart from that, Des and his wife Christina have the property "Gubbermunda" north of Roma and they buy and sell cattle here too.

So you can see that he's done just about everything one man can do at a cattle sale and he has a few stories to tell:

I saw a bullock here sold 17 times, 17 times in the one day, 17 times in 17 different pens. He started in pen 1 and finished in pen 17; he just kept jumpin' every fence and they just kept sellin' him.

In the late seventies it rained at least one day a week for seven weeks. In those days the yards were all black soil and we would scrape the mud out of the pens, it would rain again, and they were just as bad as before. They were a mess, a real bog.

Some three year old bullocks came in. They put 'em in a pen and they looked like weaners, sunk up to their bellies in the mud.

Arthur Walmsley walked into one of the big water yards in his gum boots, got bogged and struggled out without them. The boots were never found; they'd be still down there somewhere.

The Duke of Edinburgh was coming and there was a real fuss.

MI6, or some other British intelligence mob, came out and checked on all the sites where bombs could be planted. It was decreed that no person could move within five metres of the royal presence and all rubbish bins had to be removed in advance of his arrival.

The road from the yards to the highway was resurfaced, a special gate was cut in the fence and councillors and local dignitaries enacted a trial run.

They all came out in cars, drove up to Dukes Gate, someone opened a door for the "Duke", he waltzed through the gate, turned around and went back again, and that was that.

So everything was ready ... but he never came.

"Des, you've been here a long time; are you going to keep on?"

"Poverty dictates that I'll be here for quite a while yet."

Terry Ayers is the saleyards undertaker.

Like people, cattle die; some due to accidents some by natural causes and when they die they have to be buried. With around 400,000 head going through the yards each year, it stands to reason that some will end their days here, hence the need for an undertaker.

Terry and Fay Ayers operate an earth-moving business so Terry has all the equipment necessary to pick up dead animals, cart them away and bury them properly.

Sometimes he is called on by the Queensland Rail to take dead cattle from the trains for the same reason.

Mick Connell tells this story:

A cattle train travelling from the west was in trouble and the Railway rang me to see if I could help unload and take off the dead ones. I rang Terry and we went out to see what we could do.

We unloaded the wagons while Terry started hoisting out those that had died and loading them onto his truck.

We were nearly finished when the engine driver said:

"What say we leave the rest till we get to Chinchilla? The bloke down there is a mate of mine and he could do with the work."

Terry was agreeable, so we reloaded the train but left the rest of the carcases on board for the next man.

The world would be a better place if we all shared a bit more!

Wanda Fitzgerald started off by spending a couple of years in the agents' office with Pat Lenihan just on 20 years ago. She was there on Tuesdays and Thursdays, filling in the master sheets and checking off the buyers' purchases.

Wanda then worked for the Board, loading cattle out from the Tuesday store sale. She would start at 10.00am and work through while ever there were trucks to load and that often meant working all night till someone relieved her on the Wednesday morning.

"This was before we had the hut," says Wanda, "and you'd be up on the catwalk in all sorts of the weather, trying to keep your paperwork dry in the rain and at the same time making sure that the right cattle went on the right truck and the numbers balanced."

Brendan and Wanda Fitzgerald then took on the contract to weigh the fat cattle. That meant they were responsible for providing the workforce to take cattle out of the selling pens, over the scales and into the buyers' pens ready for trucking out.

As Brendan was buying most of the time, Wanda was in charge. This is how she described the operation:

We had up to 10 people, mostly men but some women too. We needed horsemen to take cattle from the selling pens to the scales, stockmen to bring them onto the scales, and others on horses to take them away from the scales to the buyers' pens.

As for me, I allocated the wateryards for each buyer and kept a list of what cattle went into each pen.

We were responsible for any discrepancies so we had to check and double check that everything was spot on before they loaded out.

I reckon the first year's contract aged me 10 years!

Actually the fat sales weren't too bad but when we got around to doing the store cattle that really tested us out.

When you weigh 10,000 stores and then go back to check the count of each lot, you find that you've been on the job for the best part of 24 hours and you're not really at your best.

I was lucky to have Trevor Brookes; he was good.

When we'd finish weighing heifers and begin on the cows, he would go off and start counting. He'd check the steers and the heifers so that by the time we finished weighing the cows, the steers and heifers would be counted and all we had to do was check the cows.

Then it was up to us to deliver the cattle.

They were long days and long nights. I remember starting at 5.00am one Tuesday morning, working straight through and finishing a 5.00pm on the Wednesday afternoon.

And as for a feed, well that was whatever we carried in the esky. We were sort of self-contained; we'd eat on the run.

In 2005 Wanda had a serious accident and ended up in hospital.

After one sale, they were moving a big line of cows. Brendan was in front opening gates and leading the way while Wanda was following behind when a couple of cows turned.

As they seemed intent on heading back, she stood aside and let them pass and continued on after the main mob.

But the two renegades changed their minds and ran back to join their mates and in doing so trampled all over the top of Wanda.

She ended up with three broken ribs and four smashed vertebrae and spent eight weeks in hospital in Roma and four weeks convalescing at home.

No one would have blamed her if she never returned to the yards but Wanda came back to see her contract through to the end.

"It wasn't an easy job," she says, "but during all the years of our contract I was very fortunate to have loyal staff, good people who understood cattle, who worked hard and who wouldn't let you down.

People like Trevor Brookes, Carey Farndon, Gordon Johnston, Jim Crane, Mandy Golden, Frank McNamara and Col Brookes; I couldn't have done it without them.

Anyway, I reckon I'd done my bit and I finished up in 2005."

Terry O'Dempsey and **Jed Taylor** are Stock Inspectors with the Department of Primary Industries and part of their job is to scrutinise the movement of stock in keeping with current legislation.

They are both senior officers. Terry has been in Roma since 1989 and Jed since 1999, so they have seen a lot of cattle and seen a lot of changes at the saleyards.

"While I was still at college I came out to do my prac work here," recalls Jed. "You'd get out here at 6 o'clock in the morning and it was that bloody cold your hands would stick to the rails when you were going round on your pre-sale inspection.

Then I'd have to sit down and write out about 80 to 100 bloody permits for the day; it was full on. It used to be a 12-hour day for us but I know some of the agents were here a lot longer than that."

"When I first came here," says Terry, "we spent a lot of time checking all the cattle for missing tailtags and then we'd sit down and issue permits for all the cattle to move out.

But with the NLIS tags, free movement across the border and travel permits generated automatically, there is no need for that.

The NLIS tags have done away with all the tail-tagging and the process is much more thorough.

The funniest thing that I've seen was the two young blokes who tried to buy a stud bull with a bottle of coins; but no doubt someone closer to the action will tell you the full story on that one."

I asked Jed if he ever got a laugh out of the job.

"It was a daily occurrence; you'd leave the office to come out here for a laugh and you were sure to get one.

I remember one time when a big line of the Tumbar weaners came down from Jericho. Mick Connell was unloading them.

I asked him if they always sent that many and he explained that it was their custom to market their annual turnoff in one hit.

Then he said: 'I do the same ... on a smaller scale!'

He's a funny bloke; he'd have three head, they had 1800!"

I asked them about their relationship with vendors and agents.

"I think we get on pretty well with everybody and that includes the Board," said Jed, "but sometimes you'll find people with opposing views; on the NLIS tags for instance.

The agents were probably the meat in the sandwich on that one early in the piece. From our point of view, we just needed to see the job done. The Board had their point of view, the agents had their position, the industry was divided, there was a fair amount of angst, but for the most part it worked and today it's part and parcel of doing business out here.

Apart from the opposing views, the commitment on the part of everybody here at the saleyards to try to make the whole thing work, was bloody excellent, it really was."

Col Brookes started working at the yards in November 1976 and 31 years later he's still here and thriving on it:

During that time I had twelve months off; I cracked up, wore out in the hips, could hardly walk, so I called it a day. They put on a send-off for me, shouted a few beers, gave me a watch and that was that.

I was on crutches for a while but they give me two new hips and once I got right I wanted to work again so I came back.

At that stage Wanda and Brendan Fitzgerald had the contract to weigh and deliver the cattle. They couldn't get anyone to handle the deliveries. I wasn't sleeping real well, so I offered to do the late shift.

When one of Wanda's boys was hurt in a rodeo accident and she went to Brisbane with him I told her not to worry about the letting out, I'd do the lot, and I did.

We never had any problems; they were very good to work for. I did it for three years and lost one beast, there was one we just couldn't track down, one beast out of about a million. Not too bad, eh?

But let's go back to the beginning.

When I first started we'd take delivery of all the cattle. We'd kick off at 2 o'clock on Monday afternoon and knock off at 11 o'clock on Tuesday morning. For that we got $35 a sale.

Leading up to one sale, Main Roads had the Mitchell Road cut off and there were trucks held up everywhere so Val Harms organised a special train to go to Mitchell to bring the cattle in.

Just as the train left town, Main Roads opened the road and let the trucks through. Who paid for the train? Don't ask me!

It used to rain in those days. One wet sale I left just on dark to do the 70km to get home and it took me 24 hours.

Duncan Creek was a banker. I curled up in a blanket on the front seat of the truck to wait for it to go down, but when I woke in the morning there was water all around me.

Eventually it dropped enough to get across but I was blocked again at the Yalebone.

My neighbour came up behind me in a Volkswagen and we waited there till mid afternoon when it looked like raining again so we reckoned we'd give it a go with the car tied on behind the truck.

We got through alright but the Volkswagen floated up and under the truck and dented the bonnet.

Muckadilla Creek was a mile wide and I couldn't cross it but I had a horse on the back of the truck so I reckoned I would ride home.

So I unloaded the horse and rode home and the wife wanted to know who this fella was riding down through the paddock.

Another time Dalgetys brought me in on Sunday night because they had a lot of cattle coming in early. But nothing arrived.

About 4.00am the first truck came and from then on they just kept comin'. From 4 o'clock till 11 o'clock I never stopped unloadin' cattle; never had a feed or a drink, it was non-stop, and there was no where to put 'em all, but somehow we managed.

In those days there were six agents, two drafts and 40 water yards and when we had those 10,000-head sales things got a bit tight.

Charlie Cosgrove and I worked well together. We had three unloading points; Charlie did all the countin' and I did all the walkin'.

Our first accommodation was a little old grader-driver's caravan which was a bit cramped, and then we graduated to the one-room steel hut which was a lot better, now we've got the high-rise air-conditioned unit which is great.

I think that's a good example of the way things have improved.

Years ago they put the hay feeding out on contract. I did that, but they stipulated that the hay had to come from Primaries.

For a big store sale in the middle of summer, I'd go down to the railway, get 110 bales of hay out of a rail wagon and put 'em in my truck, cart that load back here to the yards, throw it out to the cattle and go back and get another 110 bales … on my own!

I'd do that three times a day. You know, it gets pretty hot in the middle of summer, but I was a lot younger and a lot fitter then.

I remember one sale here, Des Cherry was selling and he had a helluva good run of cattle and he was goin' like a cut cat.

In those days we had to get in the pen and brand every beast sold with these little short brands and we were about two pens behind him so I yelled out for him to steady up.

And he just laughed and kept on goin'.

But I got square a week later. He had another good run of cattle and he was going well till he got to the end of the race and looked back, expecting to see us two pens behind, but I was sitting on the rail in the next pen waiting for him and it knocked him down flat.

I've seen some good agents and I seen some ordinary ones.

In the cattle slump Val Harms was the Winchcombes manager and they wouldn't give him any labour so I used to help him do his drafting in between unloading trucks. $10 a night I got for that.

I seen him draft 700 head here one night and he never wrote a thing down. When he finished he told me to wake him at 4 o'clock in the morning but when I got there he was already bookin' em up.

He was a helluva good agent. He was phenomenal!

Then they let out the rail truckin' on contract and I got the contract for doin' that too.

Before I took over, the agents all used to have a go. They'd bring one lot down and put 'em on front of the train, but the next lot had to go at the back, so they'd shunt the train, back and forward till the job was done. It would take hours.

The shunters used to bring a six pack with 'em every night.

Anyway they gave me a go and I lined all the cattle up in the same order as the wagons before the train arrived.

So we loaded the first wagon and the shunters knocked the top of a stubby and squatted down on the ground.

"Next wagon," I yelled. They jumped up, mumbled something like, "Stuff you blokes," and never bothered to bring six packs again.

Anyway I did those sort of things till I couldn't do them any more, but after I had my hips done I came back.

I started with Wanda and Brendan but when the Board didn't renew their contract I was looking for something to do.

During the twelve months I was away, my son Trevor took over the deliveries. He wanted to move on so I returned to that role. I was back to where I started in 1976!

But I was feeling good, I was capable of more work and I found it with Frasers, loading out their trucks working for Melissa.

So that's what I do now.

The agents are responsible for all cattle coming in and the Board is responsible for all cattle going out; Trevor Beck and his crew attend to all that.

On Mondays I work for the agents taking delivery of all the cattle, on Thursdays I'm part of the painting team, and on Tuesdays, Wednesdays, Thursdays and any other day I load out Frasers cattle.

I've sold my place and I've moved into town and a beautiful home with a swimming pool. I'm a lot closer to the job, it doesn't take me 24 hours to get home any more, so I'm getting more sleep and I like the work I do and the people I work for.

I'm 72 now, 73 in November but I feel good, I'm enjoying the life all over again and I've never been happier; I'm real happy. This'll do me till I die and they cart me off in a box.

If you like a job it's always a lot easier to do. I was brought up on the principle if you do a job, do it properly or don't do it at all.

I do like the job here: it's been very good to me and I like to think I've been very good for it too!

There is no doubt about that, Col. All the best for the future!

Kay Wilson worked for Wanda Fitzgerald for nearly three years, riding a horse and delivering cattle off the scales into buyers' pens.

"I enjoyed my time at the yards," she says. "We had some long days and a few long nights too, but we made our own fun and just kept going till it was over.

On one occasion I started at 6.00am on the Tuesday and stopped at 8.30am on the Wednesday. It was not a happy night and it was a bit too much for some of the others but Gordon Johnston and I were there with Wanda right to the end.

I had three horses that I fed on hay and changed them over every four hours. As for myself I had a bit of tucker in an esky and during the night someone shouted a Big Mac that tasted bloody good.

Very late one night we all had a laugh when my big bay mare put one of the agents up the rails.

The weighing was still in progress, I was penning up, truckies were loading out, everyone was getting a bit tense, and I had just closed the gate on one lot and was waiting for the next when the agent walked down the lane in front of me.

He had been working all that day as well as most of the night before so he would have been more asleep than awake; I don't think he even knew I was there.

Anyway, the horse snorted about a metre behind his left ear!

Now this bloke's not real agile, but he got such a fright he flew up the rails as though propelled by an explosion, I burst out laughing and we all had a bit of fun at the poor bugger's expense.

He didn't take too kindly to it at the time, but there was no harm done and later on when he settled down, he could see the funny side of it too.

These things happen at the saleyards!"

Trevor Beck agreed to work at the yards for three weeks in February 1993 … and he's still here.

In '93, Keith Kimlin was running the show, his right-hand man John Bale wanted to take time off, and so Trevor agreed to fill in.

Now Trevor has inherited Keith's old "Foreperson" portfolio and he lives in the house on top of the rise where Keith used to live.

A new position, Chief Executive Officer, has been created and Trevor reports to the present CEO, Richard Brittain.

I'll let Trevor tell you about his saleyard experience:

I had no experience with stock when I first came here. The likes of Doug Wilson, Dave McKay, Johnny Bale and Kenny Krienke taught me enough to stay alive by staying clear of runaway animals.

We were pretty busy when John came back. The drought was on, there were lots of cattle, there was plenty to do and so they kept me on as an extra. There was Johnny, Murray Guymer and me

I think Keith was happy enough, the Board was happy, and when John Bale decided to retire I received a letter from the Board to say that I was a full time employee.

I'm a bikie; I wear a beard and ride a Harley Davidson. I'm an ex oil patch man, hardly the ideal experience for a job here, but thanks to those who knew what to do, I learned from them and survived.

Doug Wilson used to say, "Never trust a cow. If a beast ever knocks you down you can bet it will be a cow rather than a bullock. A bullock closes his eyes before he hits you but a cow will keep hers open to make sure she doesn't miss."

Dave McKay told me the same thing and he and Doug are the only two blokes that I've seen that could actually turn a cow around with their bare hands. I've heard about it plenty of times but I actually saw them do it with my own eyes.

Ben Cowley
David Grimison Transport
Wagga Wagga NSW

Fergus Williams, Roma Q
Livestock Transport Pioneer
(Qld Country Life Photo)

Neil McIntosh
Lightning Ridge, NSW

Craig Dillon
Yunta Transport, SA

Gary Athorn Livestock Transport
Cunnamulla Q

Scott Henry
Curley Cattle Transport
Cloncurry Q

Melissa Jensen
Frasers, Roma Q

Morrie Troy
Gilberts Transport
Toowoomba Q

Robert Walker

Hornicks, Injune Q

Tommy Grace
Ex Lighthouse Transport
At the Cattlemans Bar at the Ekka

Peter Green
Roma Q

Ross & Donna Fraser (Frasers),
Jill & Jim Baker (Lighthouse)
When Jim Baker retired he sold out to Frasers

Liam Dunn
Frasers, Roma Q

Des Jones
Jones Bros, Injune Q

Bruce Riehl
Robertsons Transport
Toowoomba Q

Keith Aisthorpe
Roma Q

Daryl Brooks
Brooks Transport, Charleville Q

Mick Johnson
Dulacca Transport, Wallumbilla Q

Mick Goodchild & Grant Sullivan
Porters, Roma Q

Priddles Transport, Springsure Q

Cavanaghs, Inverell NSW

Doyle Campbell
Hornicks, Injune Q

David Scott
Scotts Haulage, Roma Q

Kevin Johnson
Livestock Carrier, Roma Q

Kurt Bonsey
Porters Transport, Roma Q

John Butler
Frasers Transport, Goondiwindi Q

John Barron
Steve Godsell Transport, Augathella Q

Tanami Transport, Alice Springs NT

Bill Taylor & Mick Johnson
Injune Co Freighters / Dulacca Transport

Tim Steffensen
Robertsons Transport, Taroom Q

Graham "Gidgee" Johnson
Johnson Bros, Tambo Q

Andy Douglas
Douglas Transport, Roma Q

Don & Kim Noon
"Cedarvale" Mitchell

Kevin Oldfield
"Clayton" Marree SA

Allison & Bevan Doyle
"Tumbar" Jericho

Mark Cook, Gerald Dayes & Nick Holman
GRM International men representing
"Rosewood Station" Kununurra WA

Les & Dawn Irwin with
Peter & Eileen Emery
Wallumbilla

Dan & Kristie York
"Hyde Park" Wallumbilla

Robert Teague
"Nockatunga" Thargomindah

Tina & Paul Constable
"Denholm" Dirranbandi

Tom Hartley
"Coopermurra" Mitchell

John & Cathy Beitz
"Middle Ridge" Amby

Beau Gray
"Arbrach" Longreach

Lockie, Jeff, Hayley & Julie Latham
"Toomba" Dulacca

Sally, Madeline, Jeremy & Paul Kennedy
"Dunroman" Dirranbandi

Geoff Johnson
"Zeta" Alpha

David & Joan Goodman
"Eulalie" Mungindi NSW

Allen Schutt
"Ingaby" St George

Ian Murray
Kindee Pastoral Co.

Libby, Ella, Matt & Guy Walker
"Roslin" Mungallala

David Hardie
"Dumfries" Blackall

John Chandler
"Glentulloch" Injune

Fran Brownhalls
"Ryandale" Cunnamulla

Darryl Ahern
"Dungowan" Augathella

Rosemary & Bill Gallagher
"Langoora" Thallon

Suzanna & Warren Butler
"Cooraki" Surat

Heather & Bob Bowen
"Wylpena" Mitchell

Andrew Forster
"Apache Downs" Winton

Peter Davies "The Nobbies" Cloncurry
Chris Phillips, Landmark, Cloncurry

Inga Gibson
"Chudleigh Park" Hughenden

Barry Stirling & Robyn Crocker
"Wirralie" Collinsville

Maryanne Russell
"Wodonga" Mungallala

Norm Harris & Don Rayment
"Adria Downs" Birdsville

Puddy & David Chandler
"Cobbadah" Injune

James Stinson
"Moonya" Roma

Kaye & Jim Bock
"Kilto" Wandoan

The first semi-trailer in Queensland built and operated by Fergus Williams
unloading at Roma yards in 1939
(From a black & white photo supplied by Fergus Williams family)

Porters Transport modern road train

Three generations of cattlemen at Roma Saleyards

Watkins & Co selling team

Paintings on these pages are the work of Brisbane artist
Ken Casperson

Landmark in action

Braces are popular with buyers at Roma Saleyards

David Tudor
following in father's footsteps

Ron Bahnisch "Cerberus" Marlborough
and Alan Acton "Wilpeena" Dingo

Alan Seawright
Glengraco Grazing, Yuleba

Andrew & Tania Mackenzie
"Eulorel" Surat

Renee & Dan Radel
"Burenda" Augathella

Helen & Peter Clarke
"Kentara" Condamine

Ian & Laurel Cornford
Cambooya

Herbie Neville, Alice Springs, with
Matthew Braitling "Mt Doreen" Alice Springs

Michael Barron
Roma

James Brosnan
Theodore

John Clothier
Moura

Col Henry
"The Peaks" Wandoan

Ian Robertson
"Struan" Comet

Jan Clark and John Robbins
Brisbane

Shane Stafford
Richmond Qld

Pat Creighton
Toowoomba

Norm Ehrlich
"Greenfields" Wandoan

Kim Mayne
"Wild Horse" Rolleston

Bruce Crichton
"Ivanhoe" Morven

Noel Slattery "Keltinda" Wandoam
with Doug Ramke, Miles

Lance Fox
"Bona Vista" St George

Phillip, Jennifer, Malcolm & Carla Crocker
"Crochdantigh" Muckadilla

Madeline, Tim, Georgie, Olivia & Scott Hall
"Mimmel" Toobeah.

Brian Leahy
"Woodlands" Jackson

Rebecca & Dean Arnaboldi
"Allanard" Jericho

Peter Wright
"Banyula" Condamine.

Damian Gould
Roma

Fay & Ranald Hodgen
"Riccatoon" Charleville

Bob Hall
"Greenmulla" Quilpie

Bill Moller "Spoonbill" Clermont with
Tod Dennis "Kurrajong" Clermont and
John Moller "Prairie Downs" Blackall

Ray Porter and Judy & Ross Powell
RJW Grazing, Wandoan

Gary Johnston
Toowoomba

Reg Beauchamp
"Stockport" Boulia

Damian Barsby
Roma

I was down the back cleaning troughs. Doug was trying to put an old Hereford cow out of the yard. She was a cranky old bitch, with curled in horns, and she charged him.

But he bounced off her head, just pushed himself away with his hands, and she came again, and he pushed her off, and that seemed to go on forever and he just kept palming her off as though she was nothin'. It was incredible to watch. In the end the cow gave up.

Another time, I saw Dave McKay do the same thing in the same yard with a Brahman cross cow. She was much taller than Doug's Hereford, but Dave handled her easily and she ended up running out of the yard as she was supposed to.

I loved old Doug. Kenny Krienke, Mick Connell, Don Turner, Jack Clanchy and Doug, they were my mentors. I knew very little about cattle but they taught me about handling cattle, told me what to look out for and what to be aware of.

Actually there were a lot of people around here that made me feel welcome, and that's what I like about the place. I came here as a stranger, a duck out of water, but I was treated as a friend and that's why I'm still here. I feel as though I'm part of the operation.

Another bloke is Des Collinson; he taught me a helluva lot about the maintenance side of things. When I think about it there are just so many great people here who have helped me.

With the Board taking direct responsibility for the weighing and delivery, we all work as a team.

There's Paul Klar, Chad McGuinn, Robby Harms and me here all the time then a dozen or more contractors come in to weigh the cattle, marshal them for delivery and load out on sale day.

Every so often, after a fat sale on Thursday afternoon, we'll all get together, men and women, and sit down and relax over a few drinks outside the canteen.

They work long hours in the heat or the cold, sometimes in the rain, and it's important that they realise their work is appreciated.

As for me, I'm in for the long haul. I get the same buzz out of going to work every day as I did the first day 14 years ago. When that stops, when I lose the love of the place, I'll think about the future, but till then, I'm here to stay!

At that stage, I changed the subject and asked Trevor about bikies, especially the several hundred he brought to the saleyards one day.

The Southern Cross Club raises funds to help kids with spina bifida.

Every year they do a poker run. A poker run is where you stop at five towns and each player collects a card. The player with the best poker hand at the finish wins the prize.

That year we went from Yeppoon to Alpha to Charleville to Roma to Goondiwindi and finished up in Boonah. There were 260 bikes and just over 300 people from all over Queensland and the prize for the best hand was $1000.

Anyway, most of them had never been to a cattle sale before so I organised for them all to come out on the Thursday morning to take in the fat sale before they left town.

The 260 bikes and 300 people in full bikie regalia turned up and swarmed all over the place. It was a real eye-opener for them … and Roma Saleyards has never quite been the same since!

By the way, the winner ended up donating the $1000 back to the kids and that year the run raised a total of $23,000 for spina bifida.

There are a lot of good bikies about and Trevor Beck is one of them!

Peter & Nikki Nichol are a couple of stalwarts that have worked at the saleyards for many years. Peter commenced in 1978 to work the scales when the liveweight selling of fats was introduced, and Nikki started writing up the delivery sheets in the agents' office in 1990.

When the liveweight selling of fats was introduced, the Board was looking for someone honest and reliable with cattle experience to work at the yards and operate the scales.

Cyril Humphreys was a councillor and he asked Peter to apply for the job. Peter applied and was chosen. That's how it all started.

This is his story:

There was much excitement. Up till then, fats at Roma were sold dollars per head, now it was cents per kilo liveweight, and every beast had to go over the scales and be weighed after they were sold.

To begin with, I drove the scales, checked the count and called out the names of the buyers over a loudspeaker so the stockmen knew what cattle were coming off the scales and where to put them.

Four or five years later, when better computers were installed, I was also required to fat score each lot for the LMAQ, Livestock & Meat Authority of Queensland, market report. But first they took me to Brisbane and trained me on fat scores so that I could do it just by looking at them from the scalehouse.

I would call out the fat score as the cattle came off the scales and the girl would punch that into the machine along with the sex and the average weight and from that the market report was produced.

In the mid-eighties my role was extended to cover the market reporting of the store sales.

Initially I had to write it all down by hand and fax it through to the LMAQ. The DPI had a fax machine in the Stock Inspectors office and I would use that.

In those days the store sales started at 11.00am and I'd follow the sale making these notes all day then break camp to have it on the fax before the DPI office shut at 5.00pm.

If the sale went too late because of numbers and I couldn't get it in by five, I would have to come back into town and do it on the Wednesday which of course was no good. It would be out of date.

I did that up until 1994 when I had to go away for an operation but the Board held the job for me. Des Collinson filled in while I was gone, and I had another go at it when I came back.

In the end I just ran out of herbs; it was me voice.

It has never been the same since the op; they stick this big tube down your neck and that sort of buggered my throat so that calling the cattle on and off the scales all day I'd finish up that I couldn't talk.

I'd get home and go straight to sleep; it was too much for me.

But I had a good time while I was there.

I think the best part was meeting different people every week at the store sale; people like the fellow from Jericho.

It was during the drought in the early nineties and I got to talking to this bloke who had been sending cattle down every week for about two months. In the end he just said:

"That's it! I've only got 4000 left; I'm not selling any more."

That story unfolded over morning smoko at Peter and Nikki's place, "Sutton Veney", half an hour from Roma up the Taroom Road.

Now let's hear from Nikki:

The job for the ladies in the agents' office is to record every transaction onto the master sheets, one for each purchaser, and check these off with the buyer before he leaves.

Over the years, this work has been performed by many of us including Pat Lenihan, Libby Tilbury, Judie Sorensen, Melissa Jensen, Therese Munro and a host of others too numerous to mention here.

One day we will be replaced by a computer, in fact a sophisticated new programme has already been installed and trialled.

But a computer doesn't know the buyers and it can't read their minds like we've learned to do. The trials ended in lengthy delays, buyers became disgruntled and there was much angst in the office.

At the time of writing, the programme has been shelved, the women are back on the job and the office is peaceful and happy again.

On a typical store sale day I arrive early, say by at least 8.30am, and get ready for the sale to start by dating a heap of master sheets and putting out our equipment including our book with all the regular buyers' details.

Once the sale starts at 9.00 am and the clerking sheets start coming over it's really full on. You just keep writing all day.

We transcribe each lot onto the master sheets – pen number, number of cattle, description, HGP status, brand, PIC number, price, agent code – using one sheet for each individual purchaser.

A buyer like, say, Kevin Healy, might buy 12 different ways so he would have 12 sheets, whereas others might buy so many cattle that they need more than one page to record all their purchases.

Once a buyer finishes, he comes and checks off. The steers are sold first and when the steers are finished there are a lot of buyers who come over to check off all at once and they're supposed to queue up.

But the sale is still in progress and there are new clerking sheets coming over all the time and they have to be written up. You can't do two things at once, that's why there are at least two of us and if we have over 5000 head, there are three.

When the auction is over it gets really hectic. Now there are a heap of people to check off, people everywhere; some are in a hurry to go; some are impatient; some don't mind waiting, and it's just a matter of getting through them all and keeping your composure.

Most of them are very good, some of them never seem to know what they're doing and it's the same ones every time, others get a bit stroppy … but I guess we all have a bad day at times

On an average store sale day with say 7000 cattle I would normally be back home by 6 o'clock, sometimes later.

There have been times with those really big sales that I didn't get home till nine or ten which makes for a long day.

But I've enjoyed it. Technology will eventually replace us but looking back I've always thought of it as a challenge, a challenge to get it right every sale, and I liked that.

Also, it took me away from the property, away from the drought most of the time, and it gave me something different to do.

It broadened my education; it taught me to read other people's writing – that was a challenge in itself.

I had trouble deciphering one pen that had been booked up three ways then crossed out and changed to five; it was a real mess.

I just put it aside and waited for the young bloke to come over and asked him to help me sort it out. He was very obliging, he knew what happened, but I nearly fell off the chair when he said:

"I can't read running writing but if you read each line to me I'll tell you who bought them."

What's the world coming to?

Anyway, as I said, I enjoyed it and I'll miss it when they finally decide they don't need us any more!

Tammy Harvey (nee Beck) started working for the Saleyards Board as soon as she left school. She recalls the job interview:

Barrie Loughnan was on the Board and he was in the room when they interviewed me. I gave my name, Tammy Beck, and he asked,

"Which Beck are you?"

"I'm Bobby Beck's daughter."

"I knew your dad when he used to cart cattle to the saleyards."

I think that helped me get the job.

That was 1990 and Tammy was 17; she stayed with the Board working at the yards until 2006. During those 16 years she was married, had a daughter named Grace, and became as indispensable as you can get to the whole saleyards operation.

This is her story:

When I first started they only used to weigh the fats. They had this really really old computer connected to the scalehouse but we battled on with that for a while.

Coming from school it took a lot of getting used to, working in the scalehouse surrounded by older men, but I learned a lot.

People like Peter Nichol, Keith Kimlin, Johnny Bale and Des Collinson were very helpful. Peter and Des taught me about cattle and fat scores so that I understood what I was punching into the computer; they were both very important people who taught me a lot.

Eventually the Board upgraded the computer system and we went with Equinox. That was a change for me, and everybody else, but it didn't take long to get used to it and it was a big improvement.

In 2001 it was decided to sell the stores by liveweight and that was a huge change, a really big thing for everybody. By comparison, weighing fat cattle was nothing.

Numbers steadily got bigger and bigger, and the hours got longer and longer. For weeks on end I worked past midnight for no extra pay; once I did 24 hours straight. I left at 5.30am, went home had a shower and changed, got my daughter ready and dropped her off to the babysitter, and was back at the yards at 6.30am.

It was hard, especially when I was there on my own, and for most of those big sales it was just me. It took its toll … but it was fun!

Next thing they introduced scanning EU cattle; that was another big change. The systems involved took a long time to implement but eventually it just became part of the business.

Then NLIS came in which was another huge change. Every beast had to have the eartag and the tags had to be read. The original scanners couldn't do the job they were supposed to and the Board put up with that for a while, but eventually they got rid of them in favour of using hand-held scanners operated by Livestock Link.

Now that I'm no longer involved, I miss it.

I miss the regulars like Val Harms, Jimmy Coleman, Pat Lenihan, John Bushell, Pat Ryan, Brian Morrissey, Micky Connell, Brendan Twidale; you just miss the contact with those sort of people.

They'd always make a point of coming in and saying hello. That's what I miss, the social contact rather than the work.

Jimmy Coleman? I was having one of many stressful days when Jimmy came in and gave me a hug that just made my day.

They realised how much work it took to do my job and they were always very grateful for that. They were like big brothers or uncles, really good people, like family if you know what I mean.

When I became pregnant, Brendan Wade came and said:

"Now Tammy you'll be having your labour right here. You won't be able to leave work, you can have the baby here but you'll have to keep going; we need you. You are not allowed to leave."

Anyway, I did what I could. I stayed right up till five days before the birth and was back two months after Grace was born. That was the best I could do.

After that, Brendan Raleigh came into the office as a weekly ritual. He always remembered my daughter's name and he would say:

"How's Grace? When are you going to have another? You can't have just one; she'll need a playmate."

I was devastated when he died suddenly; it made me very sad.

The day I left, Bruce Garvie and Rob Loughnan made the presentation and you took my photo. That was good. It made me feel appreciated for what I'd done over the years. Probably for the first time ever I felt that sense of being appreciated.

It was very touching and I could tell a lot of thought had gone into the present; it was a very nice feeling.

It's been a while now since I left but John Bushell pulled me up in the street the other day. Actually he was in his vehicle at a stop sign and he saw me and yelled out:

"You need to get back to the saleyards; we miss you terribly."

I'm not going back but what he said made me feel good, made me feel as though I had done something useful in my time out there.

Jim Crane was a school boy in Roma in 1947 when he first came to the saleyards. In those days there were two sets of yards, Australian Estates and Primaries, and about a dozen different droving plants operated out of Roma.

Jim would ride his bike out to the yards to see the mobs of cattle come in and he reckons on sale days the drovers would be perched up on the fences like crows.

When he left school he worked on various stations including "Weribone" at Surat, but when John Gallagher offered him a job on the road he jumped at the chance to become a drover himself.

Jim came back to work at Roma Saleyards in 2001 when they introduced the liveweight selling of stores.

A team of men and women, some on horses, some on foot, was required to shift the cattle out of the selling pens, onto the scales, then into the buyers' pens. Jim opted for the horse work; his job was to take cattle from the selling pens to the scales.

On a big day with 10,000 or 12,000 cattle to move, that takes a long time – all day and all night in fact.

I asked him: "What happens when it gets to midnight, you're hungry and tired, the horse is tired, and it's getting a bit chilly?"

"You change horses and keep going. It's a bit like droving; you only stop when the job is done!"

That's the attitude of the workers at Roma Saleyards!

Elwyn Brookes was a submariner in the Australian Navy before he started at the saleyards 20 years ago.

He has taken delivery of hundreds of thousands of cattle, trucked cattle out on the train and been on hand with his yellow paint brush at every pen in every sale to paint cattle out as required.

He describes that chore as "something no other bastard wants to do", which is true, so we're pleased you're on the job, Elwyn.

Louise Bennett took over the canteen when Cath Cocks retired:

"It was a hard act to follow," she says," but I've been here two years now, I've really settled in and everything's running smoothly.

I'm lucky to have good staff, the same people I started with - Pat Allwood, Eileen Hann and Susie Kennedy.

They are all reliable and friendly, they get on well with the agents and the buyers, there's a good atmosphere in the kitchen, and we all work together as a happy group.

The reputation of the steak sandwich that Cath made famous continues to grow. The secret is a constant supply of good meat and for that I rely on our local butcher, George Ladbrook.

Actually, I buy all my products locally; the bread comes from Western Bakeries and the meat comes from Ladbrook's Butchery.

If you ever get a tough steak, blame George!

We get busy at times, really very busy, but I never get stressed. I've worked it out if you keep going you come to the end and that's how we all look at it.

We are trying to provide a prompt and friendly service and I would like to think that comes across to our customers.

I'm glad I took it on; it's a business that suits me. I'll be here next week … and for a long time to come.

Brendan Fitzgerald first came to the saleyards as a drover:

I was droving cattle and delivered a mob to the saleyards on a Monday afternoon. The agent, Bob Simmons from Elders, was short of staff and he asked me to lend a hand to draft the cattle that night.

That was 25 years ago and I'm still here.

I helped Bob for a couple of weeks till all his men came back then Paul McCormack from Dalgetys asked me to do their drafting.

I took that on, haven't had a spell since, and I still do a bit of drafting for them on a Monday night … that's if I don't get caught up at the Barcaldine campdraft on a long weekend as I did last week.

Then there was the contract for weighing the cattle.

I started off working for Ron Stanford, the contractor who did the fat cattle. After a while I ran that business for him for a couple of years and when he retired, Wanda and I took over ourselves.

When liveweight selling of stores came in, there were two contracts, one for stores and another for fats. We did the fats, George and Shirley Ayers did the stores, but after 12 months we did both.

The Board does all that now, they employ the men and they have all the headaches; I'm pleased to be out of it.

When I first started to buy cattle there were blokes here that made a lot of noise, blokes who could and would handle a lot of cattle, and they'd try and stand on you, try and intimidate you; and one of those blokes was John Bushell. He was a bloke we all feared.

Anyhow, I started off buying a few for myself and feeding them at Toalki Feedlot, and then one day a bloke approached me and asked me to buy for him.

Tommy Cooper had a place here. He used to buy for people in the south and when he sold up and moved down to NSW he asked me did I want to take over a couple of orders that he had.

That's how I got into buying for others, including "Clifton Hills" south of Birdsville, and I still buy a fair few stores each year.

And of course we sell cattle here, in fact we won the major prize of $12,000 in the Special Fat Show & Sale organised by Shane Stafford when he was manager of Wesfarmers.

I was working for a bloke named Campbell Brownlie at Moira-Runda at Condamine and he had oats to spare. He suggested I put a few cattle on it and I sent down a couple of decks; they did very well and it was a pen of those bullocks that won the big money.

And I was with Don Turner for a while feeding hay out to cattle, so I've pretty well done most things around here but I've got no intention of being an agent or working in the office.

Over the years I've seen a lot of funny things, heard a lot of stories, had a lot of laughs, but the funniest thing I seen was when an agent stepped off the catwalk.

He was not a tall man but a vigorous auctioneer and he was having a bad day. Buyers had upset him, the further he went the worse they got, he's very red in the face and steam is coming out of both ears, and the buyers are giving him heaps.

This was in them old yards, before they had safety rails on the catwalks. Old mate is in a selling frenzy, he's on the end pen in the lane, the next one's round the corner, but he knocks 'em down in a rage, moves right along … drops out of sight … and the crowd roars!

Thank goodness he's a tough little bugger and he wasn't hurt.

On another occasion when David McNally was just getting on top of the knack of auctioneering, Johnny McMahon was giving him a bit of cheek at a fat sale and it was getting to McNally.

It was in one of the bottom pens in the old timber yards and eventually McNally cracked, jumped off the rail and came across the pen to come over and flatten McMahon.

I was down the other end with Bryce Hooper, there were half a dozen blokes between us and McMahon, and Bryce says to me, "By the time he gets to us he shouldn't be too hard to handle."

Anyway, Boondi Healy stepped in to prevent mayhem, McNally settled down, Blake Munro took over the selling, and life returned to normal … if there is such a thing as normal at Roma Saleyards.

I'm here every sale, fats and stores; there is always something to do, something going on, and it's become part of my life.

Back when we had that contract and thousands of cattle to manage, you'd have a late night drafting on Monday, come Tuesday morning, especially those frosty mornings, it took a bit to get going.

What I used to do on Monday nights was to read a story out of *Bloody Agents!* I'd start laughin' and go to sleep and in the morning I'd wake up happy and ready to start the day.

I make a habit of coming here with a smile.

Joan Ahern (nee Kerr) tells a story that goes back to the fifties when she was still a teenager and she and her sister, Mavis (now Mavis Graham) would walk cattle into the yards for various people.

On this day it was an Australian Estates sale and Joan was there when Billy Humphreys from Injune arrived.

He had a tie on, cuff links, a beautiful shirt and this little pair of dirty shorts.

Somebody asked: "What are you wearing shorts for, Billy?"

"I put me trousers under the wheel of the car to get it out of the bog!'

Frank McNamara is very much a local man. He was born in Injune; he lives in Roma and has worked in the district all his life. He's another of the horsemen that take the cattle to the scales.

It's very obvious he's happy doing what he's doing, you'll recognise him by his smile, but he was injured in a freak accident and we've missed him a bit of late.

Frank was in the lane riding back from the scales, Jim Crane was coming towards him with a pen of cows, Frank moved over against the rails to let them pass, but somehow a cow's hip caught Frank's left spur, twisted it and broke his ankle.

He finished up on crutches and was away from the saleyards for six months but he's back now better than ever and, if anything, the old smile has broadened.

Good to have you back, Frank.

Detective Sergeant Jim Wilby is the Roma-based officer in charge of the Stock Squad. He's been stationed here since 1985 and is often seen at the saleyards; it's part of his beat!

I asked him to tell us about his work at the saleyards and what changes he'd seen in the last 20 odd years:

Checking for stolen stock is only part of it. We also look into breaches of the Brands Act, Animal Welfare issues and the identification of cattle, previously with tailtags and now with the NLIS eartags.

There have been offences under the Stock Act and the Brands Act, we've identified stolen cattle mainly from the west, but you don't want to know names and I wouldn't tell you anyway.

We get a lot or requests from further out asking us to check certain consignments; we do that sort of thing all the time and I think people realise that the movement of all stock is under scrutiny.

Somebody is watching you, as they say.

The biggest change I've seen has been among the agents, the number of different people that have been through here and are gone.

I go back to the days of Val Harms, Ed Chambers and big Paul McCormack, when I think there were only three agencies here; now there are eight.

Murray Arthur Agencies started up, Peter Holland has his own business now, and lately we've seen Ray White and TopX open up.

I remember one sale the year I came here. It had been raining and there was water and mud everywhere. Paul McCormack was trotting behind a pen of cattle down the lane when he tripped and fell.

He was a huge man and he crashed face first into the mud.

Paul was a bloke with a sense of humour and he just stood up and said, "These things happen!" and continued on about his business.

I've had a great rapport with the agents over the years. There has never been any trouble, any differences we've had we've sorted out, and I think we all get on well.

Coming out to the yards is one part of my job that I do enjoy. I'm able to keep in touch with the industry but apart from that, I've met a lot of people here over the years and I like the friendship.

People like Mick Connell; he was here when I first arrived. He's a bloke full of knowledge; he'll help you whenever he can, and if you ask him something that he doesn't know he'll find out for you.

Agents like Mick make my job a lot easier; thanks fellas!

Sharon Wraight runs cattle, buys cattle and sells cattle, but that's not why she is vital to the saleyards operation.

Sharon is responsible for getting the clerking sheets from the auctioneers to the scalehouse and to the agents' office. Without those sheets the sale couldn't function; it's a very important job.

She has been doing this for 14 years in all sorts of weather including rain, hail and lightning, but like the Pony Express the sheets must get through.

She collects the papers from the clerks on the catwalk, brings them back to that big overhead platform, leaves the appropriate copies at the scales, then takes the rest down the stairs to the office.

"How many times a day would you use those stairs?"

"I've never counted but it's a lot. Work it out this way: I take two or three sheets at a time; I've seen Elders have up to 53 sheets … and there are seven other agents.

Yes, it's a helluva lot and I'm not getting any younger!"

People from all walks of life and from all parts of the world use the same stairs and look out over the sale from that same big platform. It is obvious to all that Sharon and her sheets are part of the operation, so invariably they stop and ask her questions.

"I have met delegates from both the Chinese and Japanese embassies, people from Finland, USA, South American countries, from New Zealand, South Africa, the UK, Russia, Denmark, literally from all over the world," she says.

"It's extremely entertaining; it's the best paid entertainment you could imagine, but actually the real entertainment is standing beside the auctioneers on the catwalk and hearing what they say under their breath, hearing what the public is not meant to hear.

I get the inside running straight from the horse's mouth, so to speak. I could write a book about the things they come out with, but that would be breaking a confidence and I wouldn't do that, and I don't repeat what I hear to anybody else either.

Overall, this is a marvellously entertaining place that gives people from around the world a clear view of our industry and a look at the real Australia.

It's good to be a part of it all … and deliver the sheets too!

Ken Harms has been at the yards feeding cattle, drafting cattle and putting them over the scales for the last 20 years, but he is only one of many Harms who have worked at the saleyards.

Years ago there was Ken's father, also Ken, and today we still have Ken's brothers Noel and Rob, while Ken's son Robbie lent a hand as a young man and is now a vet in Longreach.

Then there were Ken's cousins, the legendary agent Val Harms and his brother, the long-serving stockman Roy Harms.

Makes you wonder where we would have been without the valuable contribution of all members of the Harms family?

Pat Allwood has been working at the canteen for 19 years, first with Cath Cocks and now with Louise Bennett. This is her story:

"It's like a big family out here.

I remember when Cyril Close came to the counter one day, all smiles, to tell us his first baby was born. That was young Cody; he'd be about 11 now I suppose.

In my time lots of new agents have come here and had children, now they're at school; how time passes so fast.

You can have a joke with the men, some appreciate that, some don't, but if you were in trouble any one of them would be there to help you in a flash.

I'll never forget the day when I was unloading the milk crates and came across this dirty big green frog. I hate 'em. Anyway I let out this enormous scream and ended up on the table.

Two agents rushed in; the first one was just as scared as me and took off back out through the door but the other one, Mick Connell, took the frog out for me. Every time he sees me now he tells me there is a big green frog outside.

Mick would be the first bloke to help anyone.

Jimmy Coleman is another one; he's a true gentleman. Never cranky, always says g'day to you, always friendly, always the same. There are some really lovely men that come here."

Then she started talking about Aunty Pat's Slice, a delightful home made fruit slice that used to be served about smoko time.

I remember it well. It was in the early nineties when I was still one of those bloody agents.

I had a piece one morning; it was very nice, and I said to Pat:

"Did you make this?"

"Yes I did," she replied, tongue in cheek. "Was up all night baking the stuff and that was the only bit left. Goes off like hot cakes."

The legend was born. Aunty Pat's slice, which really came from the baker's shop, became a culinary icon at the canteen, popular with not only the workers but with tourists from around the world.

So much so that there was constant congestion in the dining area, agents and buyers had to queue to order a feed and, rather than build a bigger canteen, the Saleyards Board decreed that the delicacy be removed from the menu.

True story??

Thanks for the memories, Pat.

Chad McGuinn has been working for the Board for the past 12 months and most sales can be seen moving the cattle onto the scales.

I asked him about his job:

"This is totally different to what I've done before," he says. "I had 18 years on oil rigs before this so you can see what I mean when I say it's different.

Trevor Beck turned up and asked me to take it on. I knew Becky; he's an old oil patch man too though I didn't know him on the rigs. Anyway I reckoned I'd give it a go and I'm pleased I did.

The people make it.

Everyone's very friendly. I don't have anything to do with the buyers but the agents all say hello and the blokes I work with are easy to get on with.

A couple of times I've loaded out on weekends and I've found the truckies to be extremely good people too. Get in and give them a hand and they appreciate what you do for them.

I was brought up to go the extra yard and I've found that if you go out of your way to help someone, that extra little bit makes it easier for everyone ... and it makes the day go faster too.

Over the last couple of weeks we've been working on ways to speed up the weighing, to move the cattle through better, and that's starting to happen.

I think it's very noticeable that the weighing has gone more smoothly in recent weeks. I take a bit of personal pride in that.

They say there are some dramas here and different ones have their own agenda, but all those I work with have a positive approach and I think the whole show is working pretty well."

John Bale worked for the Board at the saleyards for 10 years during Keith Kimlin's time and no record would be complete without reference to this great little worker who's not with us anymore.

I knew him, he was still there when I arrived in 1991, but of course I didn't know him as well as Keith did, so I have left it to him to tell us what he did and how he did it:

What did he do? He did everything, literally everything!

He was basically there for general assistance and maintenance and that covers a heap of activities.

John was a skinny little bloke, about the same age as me, a good hard worker, trustworthy and thoroughly reliable; a bloke that gave one hundred percent with or without supervision. On top of that he was a good stockman and his counting was spot on.

I suppose most of us reckon we can count but counting stock is a totally different exercise to counting stationary items and not everybody is good at it.

In our job at the saleyards it was essential to be able to count cattle as they came off trucks, as they loaded out, as they were moved from one pen to another, and John Bale's count could be relied on every time.

He drove the bobcat, cleaned out the pens, fixed anything that needed fixing (that was a full time job in itself!), supervised the loading out, and when all the outside work was done and everybody had gone home, he would tidy up the canteen and clean the toilets.

And when I had to be away he would fill in for me; he was the complete all-rounder.

The saleyards tend to attract pranksters and larrikins and those types are fairly common among certain groups, but John wasn't at all like that.

He was popular but more the subdued type, a man who kept to himself and who just kept working. He was the ideal man for the job; it's a pity he got sick.

Thanks for that, Keith.

6. Buyers

Cattle buyers range from fulltime professionals to hobby farmers and include agents, cattlemen, commission buyers, dealers and just about anybody else in the industry; even the churches buy cattle at times.

At Roma, there is a band of locals that turn up at every sale whether they are buying or not; they are checking out the market, dodging work at home or have nothing better to do.

Then there are the staff buyers from registered feedlots and/or meatworks, the professional commission buyers who make a living out of buying for others, the cattlemen doing their own buying to restock with breeders, steers to fatten or little cattle to background for a specific job in the future, and often agents will act as buyers as a service to their clients.

And then there are the dealers; where would we be without them? These blokes will buy cattle today to sell tomorrow and hope for a profit. They are prepared to back their judgement that they know the market and know where they can find a buyer at a higher price.

In the past, some of them have made a fortune, some made a living and some went broke. Today, they are a rare breed, but you'll find at least a couple of them matching their wits against the world at Roma every sale. If nothing else, they put a floor in the market.

Store cattle buyers can come from as far south as Victoria when the season is favourable down there and in recent times we have seen buyers from Boulia, Richmond and Hughenden when good rain fell in North Queensland.

In brief, buyers can be anybody from anywhere.

Brendan Twidale is a buyer who has a way with words to describe cattle. Here's one of his classics:

"That steer's arse is so small you could wash it in an egg cup!"

John Matthewson is one of three staff buyers operating in Roma for "E.T." Edward Throsby, a young man who built a modern hot-boning abattoir at Singleton NSW in 2000.

John, and his mates David Tudor and Tim Perram, are young and keen salaried operators who are under instructions to shop for value on plain cows and bulls; they all preach from the same bible.

Ray Nielsen "Brunell" Morven, regarded by those who knew him as a true gentleman, bought cattle at Roma for over 50 years from the time he had a feedlot at Mt Tyson on the Darling Downs.

In later years he operated from "Brunell", attending most store sales at Roma buying mainly British cross steers to take back home and fatten before bringing them back to a Roma fat sale.

Ray left us for a better place in 2004 but his widow, Dulcie, and his sons, Garry and Glen, made this poem available and helped me to paint a picture of a bloke we all admired.

> *With fat cattle in the paddock*
> *And buffel growing tall*
> *The man they named Ray Nielsen*
> *Would be the happiest of them all.*
>
> *There's nothing he likes better*
> *Than to see his bullocks feed*
> *On lush green grass for grazing*
> *And water for their need.*
>
> *He's topped the sales at Roma*
> *Without the help of CALM*
> *Ray said: There's a place for technology*
> *But not on my bloody farm.*

Ray Nielsen stood out from the crowd; he was not your average buyer. Quietly spoken and unassuming, he was always well dressed, never forgot a name and greeted people warmly with his flashing smile, a smile that I for one will never forget.

Garry was reminiscing about coming to the sales with his Dad:

"Mum would make sure he polished his boots the night before. We'd leave early, drive down from Morven and he'd sleep all the way. When we pulled up at the yards, he'd sit up, comb his hair, put his hat on, and he'd be ready for business."

We all miss a bloke like Ray around Roma Saleyards!

James Brosnan is based at Theodore and buys for Teys Bros Biloela, Rockhampton and Beenleigh as well as their Miamba Feedlot at Condamine. He has been coming to Roma for 14 years.

"I like coming to Roma," he says. "The numbers are here so you get to buy good lines of cattle. It's a friendly place; you are dealing with genuine people and, with blokes like Jimmy Coleman and Boondi Healy about, you are guaranteed of a laugh every sale."

Malcolm & Boosie Crichton are from "Myall" Morven; her real name is Helene but she prefers to be called Boosie. Crichton families have been in the Morven district for a long time.

The dingoes ate all their sheep so now they are cattle breeders selling regularly at Roma, but in the early part of 2007 they had some good rain and decided to buy a few stores.

And so they came to Roma Saleyards.

As this buying business was all new to them, they sought advice from the market reporter who used to attend parties with Malcolm, his brother Robert and all their mates in Charleville back in 1962 when there was party in town every Friday night.

Well the market reporter discussed a few pens with the potential buyers and confused the issue to the extent they wished they had never asked him, but they must have had a win because later on when they saw him in the canteen they were all smiles, called him over and Malcolm said:

"I've got a joke for you, a good Catholic joke; you'll like this one, sit down."

I found a chair and he went on:

A nun is in a taxi and she notices the driver is constantly looking in her direction.

"Is there something wrong," she asked.

"Sister, I've always had this burning desire to kiss a nun."

"Well, if you're a Catholic and not married I suppose that would be alright."

"No, I'm not married and yes, I'm a Catholic," says the cabby.

"Okay, pull over at the park."

The taxi stops, they get out, walk over to the park bench, sit down, she throws her arms around him and lays one huge passionate kiss on him so that his knees shake and he has to come up for air.

The journey continues. Three blocks further on the driver, having recovered his breath, says:

"It's no good Sister, I feel terrible, I must confess, you see I'm a married man and I'm not really a Catholic at all."

"No worries, mate; me name's Eric and I'm on me way to a fancy dress party!"

The things you hear at the saleyards!

Keith Cameron "Ardno" Roma buys a lot of steers every year the season allows. He is definitely a local; his grandfather purchased the block for 1/5½ (2c) per acre and it has been in the family ever since.

The Camerons derive most of their income from broadacre farming but also turn over about 2000 steers a year. These have to be sourced from somewhere hence Keith was, and son Nick now is, a regular purchaser at Roma store sales.

This is Keith's story:

The liveweight scales made a big difference to our operation. Before they came in we were buying on "guessed" weight and selling on liveweight and I can assure you that doesn't work.

When I was doing the buying I reckon some of the auctioneers would have a go at me and put in a few extra bids that weren't mine and then knock them down to me anyway.

Sometimes I copped it sometimes I didn't; it depended on how badly we wanted the cattle. But these days, with this present crop of agents, they have either tidied up their act or it's not as obvious.

Once, when Brendan Wade was auctioning a line of about 200 Hereford steers from Morven, my bid didn't match the owner's expectations and he passed them in and took them back home.

The very next week Brendan took me out to the property and I offered him $20 a head less than I bid at auction and he took it.

Something must have changed!

Nick does all the cattle business these days. I still go out there and pencil for him, but most times I just go out there.

I catch up with a few mates – John Dearden, John Galwey, Tony McLennan, Graeme Sheppard and blokes of similar vintage – and we talk about the weather, the market, the bloody agents and keep in touch with what's going on about the place.

There is an atmosphere in the buyers' lane that is hard to describe; you've gotta be there. And I always have a cup of tea in the canteen; it's the most important part of the whole show.

You get to meet the buyers that have come long distances; it's surprising the people you meet.

Keith and Jenny Cameron now live in town and as the conversation about the saleyards wound down, Jenny came home and added:

When we lived on the property and Keith would go into a sale, they must have either had a helluva lot of cattle or the auction was very slow, because sometimes he didn't get home till after midnight!

Tim Perram buys plain cows and bulls for Throsbys at Singleton. Besides working the Roma sales he also buys at Longreach and Dalby in Queensland and has been to every selling centre in NSW.

Tim is a five-year veteran in the business and is bred in the purple as a cattle buyer having those great operators Harry Perram and Alec Martin as his grandfathers. And he does a great job for Throsbys.

He reckons at State of Origin time there's always a wind-up between the buyers before the game. If the Blues happen to win, next day at Roma Saleyards you wouldn't know there'd been a game, but if the Maroons get up they drive it into the NSW buyers at every pen.

Col Davis "Wamba" Chinchilla attends just about every store sale buying for his feedlot which turns off around 5000 head annually, export bullocks as well as cattle for the domestic trade.

"We need a steady supply of stores," says Col, "and what better place to shop than Roma Saleyards.

There's always plenty to choose from but you have to be here on the job; what's here this week won't be here next week.

Apart from that, it's the place to be to feel the market, to keep in touch with other buyers and to really understand what's going on."

Shane Stafford first came to Roma with Elders in 1981 and was back as the manager of Wesfarmers in 2000. These days, he and his wife Belinda have the business Stafford Stock & Property in Richmond and it was in that role that he was back as a major buyer in 2006.

"In my time in Roma as an agent," remembers Shane, "after canvassing for buyers prior to sale without much luck, you would find 8000 cattle penned up at 8.30am on a Tuesday morning, the carpark would be sparsely occupied, and you'd be wondering what was going to happen to the market.

But then someone would turn up from somewhere - Forbes, or Condobolin, Wandoan, Bathurst or the Channel Country - and we'd get away with it once again.

That's the thing about Roma; the cattle can come from anywhere in Australia but so too can the buyers. I can't remember ever having what you might call a 'bad' sale."

In 2006 while the drought roared on in southern Queensland, most parts of The North received good rain and Shane just happened to be the "someone from somewhere" who saved the day.

Three times he came down from Richmond with orders from R.G. Keats & Co "Cassilis" Richmond and Pensini Grazing "Culloden" Muttaburra and on each occasion he was the big buyer on the day taking home 632, 1484 and 546 head.

Thanks for comin' Shane!

Michael Barron was an auctioneer with Primac when he first came to Roma from Toowoomba in 1992. These days, and for the past 10 years, he has been a buyer:

"As an agent in the early nineties I bought quite a few cattle for various clients and feedlots and those people stuck with me when I went out on my own," he says.

"Terry Nolan at Wide Bay Feedlot over near Gympie is one; another is Adrian Harvey down at Hay in NSW; then there is John Lloyd at Wieambilla Feedlot at Condamine; ACC here in Roma; and in more recent years David Connolly at the AA Company has had me buying for them.

I buy on a commission basis and over the years I've been lucky enough to be able to build up a healthy little business.

I also buy cattle in my own right so one way and another I'm here at Roma every sale

We live on 1000 acres just out of town. Roma is central to all our activities, it's a good place to raise a family, my family is here, our business is here, and we like it here. We're here to stay.

And the saleyards! Well, you come out here on business but it's a day out. There is always a bit of news, a bit of fun; someone's always having a joke; that's the way the saleyards scene works.

I'm a part of all that and I wouldn't miss it for quids!"

Damian Gould is the Roma based buyer for AMH, Australia Meat Holdings, the biggest beef processor in Australia and now part of JBS Friboi the largest meat processing company in the world.

His first taste of the saleyards was as a 10-year-old drafting cattle at Wandoan and helping his father, legendry agent Lee Gould.

How did he become a meat buyer?

"It just sort of happened," says Damian. "I went to college then worked on cattle properties in Zimbabwe and did some buying there; I was buying feeder steers for a grazier who had feedlots.

When I came home AMH had an ad in the paper looking for a cadet buyer. I applied, got the job and started at Dinmore. I was 21.

I had twelve months at Dinmore, one month at our Prime City feedlot at Beaudesert, six months in Townsville, six months in Roma, and then I was posted to Blackall where I spent seven years.

Working out west was a learning experience for a young fella. Coming up against the likes of Pluto Tudor and Boondi Healy every sale at Longreach was a bit daunting at first, there were good times and bad, but it was all part of a buyer's education and I learned plenty.

When Scotty Sheehan transferred to Townsville I came here to take his place and I'm well settled here now. We have a little place at Amby where I live with my family, we are happy here and I'm not going anywhere.

Roma is a good, strong area. Right now we are in the middle of a rip-roaring drought yet it's surprising just how many cattle are there to be bought … and when it rains there'll be even more cattle.

I'm very very happy to be here and we're very settled here."

And we're happy you're here too, Damian.

Col Henry "The Peaks" Wandoan is a regular buyer.

"When the season allows, I buy store cows to fatten," says Col. "I used to buy cows & calves but these days I stick to cows but I haven't been able to buy for the last three months.

I've been coming for 40 years and seen all the changes. It's a great set up, the whole place is very well run, you can buy whatever you like and you get a good feed.

I've heard a few jokes, seen a few blokes do their lolly, but 99% of the people are happy. You can't get better than that!

And when it rains, I'll be back!"

Terry Lanskey comes from Elders Meandarra; he's been coming to Roma to buy cattle with his clients for 30 years.

"We mainly buy good quality lightweight steers that we grow out to around 480kg to go into the feedlots," says Terry.

"In normal years we would source up to 10,000 head out of Roma and when our season turns around we'll be back in the market providing suitable cattle are available.

I enjoy coming here. You catch up with old mates, you find out what's going on, and you have a day out whether you buy cattle or not, and of course Roma is great place to do your grocery shopping.

Back in the old days there'd be a carload of clients and you'd find it was a long trip home through Surat and Glenmorgan, but these days it's hard to find a designated driver so we get home a lot quicker.

Noel Slattery "Keltinda" Wandoan has been coming here regularly every Tuesday for 12 years and on and off for 10 years before that:

"I buy for certain agents in Coonamble, Tamworth, Narrabri and other parts of NSW and Victoria, and now and again I buy a few for myself," is how Noel summed up his activities.

"I would buy 30,000 to 40,000 cattle a year and half of those would come out of Roma Saleyards.

It's a good day out; what else would you do on a Tuesday?

This is the place to be. There are always big numbers of cattle, there are all types to choose from, and if you can't buy cattle you can have a good yarn.

Every time you come here you go away knowing more than when you arrived. It a great place to source cattle but it's also a great place to find out what's going on."

Terry Ryan is with Landmark at Chinchilla. An experienced agent, auctioneer and cattle buyer, Terry has been coming to Roma since the early eighties:

"In the past I have been invited to lend the local Landmark team a hand by selling the cattle, but most weeks I'm here at the store sale with orders to buy for my clients."

I asked him to recount some of his memories:

"The sale that sticks in my mind was in the old timber yards in the early eighties. It was very dry all over Queensland and NSW and the yarding was something like 14,000; there were cattle everywhere!

In those days the store sale didn't start till 11.00am and this one finished under lights at about 9 o'clock at night.

By late afternoon, people were getting very short on the ground then the shops shut in town and more people came out for a look and swelled the crowd.

The market held up pretty well all day but when it got dark it started to rain and continued to rain quite heavily through to the end. That sort of weeded out the onlookers.

But we hung on and got wet and around half past eight we were lucky enough to buy a big lot of 80 cows & calves for $180; that's 80 cows and 80 calves at $180 cow & calf. Very good buying!

That was one of the bigger days and it turned out well for us.

It's a long day to be here from the first pen of steers to the last pen of cows & calves but, no matter what sort of cattle we want, we can normally find our requirements out of a Roma yarding.

But it's a pretty enjoyable day; we are only two hours down the road, there are not too many Tuesdays that I miss, and if you do happen to miss a couple of weeks, people ask where you've been as though they thought you'd dropped off the twig.

It's a great cattle-selling centre. I reckon on average we would buy around 200 head a sale, say 8-10,000 a year but, apart from that, you meet a lot of people and even when I don't buy cattle I do other business just by talking with people in the lanes.

I like coming to Roma and I'll be back again next week!"

John Brodie "Boorameel" Condamine has been coming to Roma as a buyer since 1990. He would probably buy 3000 to 4000 steers a year, mostly crossbred flatback types to take home to finish on crop.

But on occasions he has been known to back his judgment and buy anything that looks like returning a quick profit.

On one occasion a big line of Santa Shorthorn cross cows & calves from South Australia came in too late for the store sale on Tuesday so they were put up in the fat sale on Thursday.

The cattle had come from drought-stricken country, the cows were in plain store condition, the calves had not been mothered, and they put them up as pens of cows and pens of calves.

Half a dozen blokes smelled a bargain and turned up to buy a pen or two but John Brodie bought the lot … every pen of cows and every pen of calves … and trucked them all to Boorameel.

The pundits reckoned he was crazy. They reckoned half the cows would die and what calves survived would be stunted orphans.

A week later I saw John at the saleyards and I asked:

"How did you get on?"

"Well I put 'em all on a failed grain sorghum crop and as far as I can tell all bar two of the calves are getting a drink."

He bought 442 calves that day and a similar number of cows.

Three months later he re-offered the 440 weaners through a Roma store sale and they made as much as he had paid for the cows and calves; so he got the cows for nothing.

"Would be nice to do that every year," was all he said.

John's not a loudmouth or a bignoter; he just goes about his business but he brings his own brand of humour to the yards.

I was beside him one time in the cow & calf run when they came to a small pen of undersized Murray Greys that the auctioneer was raving on about and telling us how good they were then adding that the lady who owned them was on hand to see them sold.

"I hope she's not a heavy drinker," was John's quiet comment said in such a way that no one else heard.

And apart from doing business there are other attractions:

"I come here every week. I like talking to people and even if I don't buy I keep in touch with what's going on. I do a bit of shopping in town, attend to other business, have a feed at the canteen; it's the day in the week that I bring myself up to date with the industry."

Damian Barsby is the Manager Store Stock for Australian Country Choice (ACC) and based at their Brindley Park Feedlot, Roma. He has been in that position for eighteen months; before that he had eight years with the same company in the abattoir at Cannon Hill.

He is at Roma every Tuesday buying 200-400 stores for Brindley Park and now that he has fully settled in to his new role I asked him what he thought about Roma:

"Great place for the family, good place for the kids, but out here at the saleyards the bloody agents love to give you a touch up.

The auctioneers, they're all at it, all prepared to have a bit of a go," he said with a broad smile, "but there's nothing wrong with putting a bit of spirit into the job and if I can catch 'em at it I'll pull 'em up. At the end of the day we all get on pretty well."

Gary Johnston is the Teys Bros Toowoomba based buyer who comes to Roma for the fat sale every Thursday and who has been coming out here for the last couple of years.

He started as a cadet buyer with Fields and later worked with Gilbertsons, but since 1990 he has been a Teys Bros man.

I asked him what he liked about coming to Roma:

"You know when you come here you can get your teeth into a good number of cattle, they are sold in big pen lots, and they get through them pretty quickly," he said.

"As far as the people are concerned I guess they are typical of the group you'd find at most saleyards; they have a sense of humour, it's a competitive but friendly atmosphere, and you can enjoy the day as well as do business.

I like coming here. Saleyards buying is much more fun than buying over the phone. I've been in the job since 1969 and absolutely love it as much now as I did back then."

Pat Creighton buys for Bindaree Beef and is based in Toowoomba. He comes to Roma twice a week and has been doing so for the past three years.

This is what he had to say about the saleyards:

I like coming here because there are so many cattle to pick from, good cattle too. And the best part about it, every week is different.

You're not looking at the same cattle or the same people or anything the same two weeks running; that's what I like about it.

7. Characters

No matter where you are - on the beach at Caloundra, in a pub in Brisbane, on a tour bus in France, anywhere in the world - you mention the word 'saleyards' and someone will say 'characters'.

The words are synonymous; saleyards and characters, they go hand in glove; wherever there are saleyards there are characters; it's as though saleyards are breeding grounds for these people.

And it's no different at Roma; the only problem here is to work out who to include in the few pages available.

Val Harms is not with us anymore but no account of Roma Saleyards would be complete without mention of this great agent, cattle buyer and genuine real-life character.

I didn't know him as well as others who have been here longer, but I was fortunate that he allowed me to write this little story for Blue's Country Magazine:

Val's forebears came to the Maranoa in 1880 and as a 68 year old veteran of the saleyards you would have to say he is well known, probably the best known identity at Roma Saleyards, the biggest cattle selling centre in Australia.

He started work with the private agent Dick Condon before he was old enough to have a driver's licence.

Condon sold out to Winchcombe Carson, Val worked his way up to become the Branch Manager of Winchcombes, held that position for 18 years then stuck with the business when it became Dalgetys.

In a career spanning 45 years and 3 months he was always an agent in Roma except for an 11 month stint at Wallumbilla.

Val made his mark in the industry when Roma was Hereford country. He specialised in the breed, bought and sold thousands of them, advised stud breeders about them, purchased hundreds of bulls for clients, and earned the title, "Mr. Hereford."

Now retired from active agency work, Val keeps in constant touch with the market. He attends every sale and keeps his hand in buying stores, predominantly Herefords, for friends and contacts in the three Eastern States.

"Many of the people I buy for I've never met; I've been buying for some of them for 20 years and never had a row," says Val.

The other week he lined up a four deck consignment of Hereford steers from "Durham Downs". Once he had the first pen knocked down to him as "Dals Roma No.1" at $400 there was no stopping him and he finished up with the lot.

"Who did you buy those for?"

"Mind your own business," was the reply.

That's Val!

That's what I wrote for Blue's in September 2004. I'm also aware that Val is mentioned several times in various stories in this book already, but to give him his due as Roma's longest serving agent ... and a character ... I asked Murray Arthur to add his comments:

I was with Dalgetys in Mitchell when Val was with Dalgetys in Roma. We would introduce a lot of cattle into Roma and there was no doubt in anyone's mind that Val was in charge of our saleyard operations.

I vividly recall booking cattle in with Val. He insisted that the description and everything be spot on and you were soon put in your place if the cattle did not measure up to the details given.

He had a way with words, very much to the point, and the way he conveyed his massage ensured that you remembered it next time.

Val insisted on perfection in the presentation of cattle, the way they were drafted, where they were penned, it was very important to him; and he developed a clientele that would sell nowhere else but with Val. He commanded a tremendous amount of respect.

Val wasn't backward in coming forward; he let you know where you stood. Up on the catwalk he had that big rough exterior, he wasn't an auctioneer he just ran the show, but when you got him down on the ground and you got to know Val, he was as soft as butter.

Pat Clarke – ringer, drover, roughrider, cattle buyer, grazier, horse trainer, but above all a dealer, one of the best, and another one of those characters that has gone to that big saleyards in the sky.

Pat came from Bellbrook down in NSW. At 16 years old he sold his pony for £20 ($40) and left home.

He found work on Tooloombilla north of Mitchell then on Merrivale at Injune before droving with Alban Knaggs to bring cattle down from Springsure to Singleton and all stops in between.

Next it was the rodeo circuit and Pat did well enough to make a living out of it for 5 years so he would have been right up there with the champions.

His next career move was to go droving in his own right. Jack Smyth provided a £250 ($500) loan so Pat could buy his own plant at Goondiwindi and Pat shifted cattle for Jack and other dealers and also for the Buffier family who were based at Maitland.

Wally and Keith Buffier handled cattle by the thousands and it didn't matter where they were. Pat started out droving for them then became responsible for organising the movement of all their cattle and eventually started buying for them.

One day he bought 250 head at Inglewood. "I bought 'em because they were cheap," said Pat.

"Where are you sending them?" asked Wally.

"Well I haven't thought about that yet," replied Pat.

"I'll tell you what. Never buy another beast if you don't know where you're going. Forget it; go to the races instead!"

Pat described that as the most valuable lesson he ever learned.

Another time when Pat bought 1200 Mt Howitt bullocks the pick of 5000 for eighteen quid ($36) and sent them to agistment at Moree the Buffiers put him in for a third share of the profits and that gave him the start to kick off on his own.

After that he handled a lot of cattle, up to a thousand cattle a week, all over Australia - he bought cattle in Melbourne and Cloncurry and sold them at Goondiwindi; cattle from Derby he sold at Katherine - and he was welcomed back time and again to do more business, in fact the Garlands at "Innisvale" Injune sold their Hereford weaners to him for 40 years.

Pat drew "Biddybrook" Moonie in a Land Ballot in 1967, bought "Foxborough" at Westmar in 1972, and also owned a couple of small blocks of good country handy to Goondiwindi and Boggabilla.

He had racing stables and trained horses but would rather go to a cattle sale than spend a day at the races.

Pat came to Roma Saleyards hundreds of times over the years and bought thousands of cattle. He is mentioned elsewhere in this book and you gain the impression that he is remembered as a big operator, a real character and a true gentleman.

Peter "The Feather" Knauer started buying cattle at Roma in 1957. Before that he worked all over Australia.

He was a jackaroo at "Albinia Downs" Springsure, overseer on "Kolendo" SA, a porter on the Railway in Cairns and a stablehand for Jim Cummins, the father of Bart Cummins, in Adelaide.

He worked on a fat lamb property at Mt Gambier, was a bar steward for the Yacht Club in Perth, then leading hand in the cheese factory at Kempsey where he played A Grade Rugby League in the Central Coast competition during winter and was a lifesaver and member of the boat crew for Crescent Head SLSC in the summer.

Peter began as a stock salesman with AML&F at Dalby in 1956 but after a couple of months had to go into National Service. Moving around Australia he had previously missed out, so he went into Wacol for three months, completed his National Service, then went back and got stuck into the business.

Let him tell the story:

In those days the Darling Downs was mainly fat lambs and vealers and there were very few good herds of beef cattle. So I made up my mind then to develop a business based on quality Hereford cattle sourced from Mitchell, Injune, Roma and Wallumbilla, from the Maranoa so to speak.

I bought all the cattle I could out of the paddock, as well as the saleyards, concentrating mainly on steers but handling cows, heifers and cows & calves as well. I did about 1000 head a week!

We had a nucleus of clients but there wasn't really enough of them to take all the cattle I bought, so I punted them.

Any cattle I traded through Dalby saleyards were mine, with any cattle to Goondiwindi there was Pat Clarke and myself, and once they went over the border there was Pat, Jack Smyth and me. That was the arrangement we had for many years.

I got to know Jack when I tried to buy the "Forestvale" steers.

I put in an offer of £12 for them only to find that Jack had offered £12.50 and they had accepted his price.

I rang him and asked if he would take a profit on the deal. He thought about that for a while then said:

"No I won't take a profit but I'll tell you what I'll do; I'll send 'em to you and you can sell 'em for me."

And that's how the association with Jack got started.

I can't remember how many times I went to Roma over the years, it would have been thousands, but I do vividly recall the people who frequented the sales and some of the antics they got up to.

There was Wally Humphris "Wealthy Wal", Doug Heelan who used to buy for Andersons and a dealer named John Fullerton-Smith. He was always whingeing about the money he'd lost on the last lot of cattle while at the same time busting to have a go at the next lot. We called him John Fulltime-Smith.

But apart from all the fun and games we did serious business and helped a lot of clients.

People like McInnerney Brothers for instance; they were dairy farmers with a place at Irvingdale when I went to Dalby.

I bought a lot of cattle for them over the years and they did well. They went through the slump in '74 of course and that hurt everyone. To give you an idea we got down to selling at 20c/lb dressed weight and restocked at $30 a head.

But when the market recovered they got all their money back, plus a bit more, and went on to expand their operation. Today they run five properties from Glenmorgan to Stonehenge.

I like to look back and think that to culture clients like that is a bit of a success story.

I asked him about nicknames, in particular "The Feather".

Well Pat Clarke was "The Ant" firstly, then "The Black Ant".

You remember those saleyard sandwiches cut into four? Well, like an ant, Pat would take one little pick out of the centre and throw the rest away. So they called him "The Ant" to start with.

I don't know who said it first, might have been Bushell, but as Pat was dark it later changed to "The Black Ant" and he was known as that all over the place.

In my case "The Feather" came about during a conversation at a sale and the name stuck.

Bill McKay and Jack Smyth had the whole Mitchell area tied up; they bought all the cattle.

Bill's brother Barney had a place at Macalister and he was at the Dalby yards one day, just having a look, when we had Roma cattle there and I was doing the selling.

Someone asked Barney what he thought of me and he replied:

"Oh, he's nearly honest."

To which the other bloke said:

"So you'd call him a feather; wouldn't give you a hard touch."

And that was it and I became "The Feather" and as far as I know, I still am to many people.

In 1957 Peter started buying at Roma Saleyards, that's 50 years ago as this book goes to print. You don't see him at the sales these days but when they ask for the buyer's name you often hear "Success Pastoral".

That's Peter's company. He operates from his office in a high rise unit at Kangaroo Point in Brisbane. Someone else may be doing the bidding but The Feather is still calling the shots.

Ken Wormwell uses a walking stick these days but not so long ago "KD" drafted all the cattle for the agents in the old Roma saleyards and matched it with the best as a horseman, cattleman, grazier, drover, roughrider, campdrafter, show judge, cattle buyer, contract musterer and station manager.

As a drover he worked for Forrester & Buffier, Geoff Killen, Australian Estates, Elders, Tancreds and others and at one time had four plants and 6500 bullocks on the road all at once. He would have run one of the biggest contract droving operations in Australia.

One job in early 1964 involved taking 1350 Austral Downs steers from Winton to Singleton for Harry Perram; after 29 weeks on the road the cattle arrived fat, the agents put on a party in Newcastle and "KD" showed slides depicting the various stages of the journey.

Thirty-six hours later at Cunnamulla he took delivery of 2000 cows & calves headed for South Australia via Nockatunga. You could say he spent a bit of time on the road!

As a campdrafter he is ranked among the champions. He won the Marie Downs Gold Cup, the Chinchilla Grandfather Clock and in a Novice draft at Tara riding five different horses he won first, second, third and fourth prizes, plus the special trophy for a maiden horse scoring the highest points – in other words, he won the lot.

Ken bought cattle for the likes of Jack Smyth, S.F. Falkiner, Peter Bailleau and George Crouch from Sydney for whom he operated for 4½ years. In one six month period he bought George 12,000 mixed sex weaners out of Roma, Injune, Taroom and Wallumbilla.

Ken managed "Meeleebee Downs" at Wallumbilla for the late Bob Freeman. On one occasion he organised the sale of 1400 Meeleebee steers and heifers in a Roma sale and another time, when buying for Freeman, Ken purchased what was then a record number in one day by any buyer with a single order - 1207 Hereford steers.

A real bush character, he describes himself simply as "a happy-go-lucky bloke who loves working with horses, cattle and fair dinkum people."

If you want to know more and have the time to listen, you'll sometimes find him perched on a rock under one of the Athel Pine "Trees of Knowledge" at the saleyards.

Stop for a yarn; he'd love to tell you the full story.

Wallace Logan came to Roma as a buyer, a big buyer.

Wallace owned a lot of country and ran a lot of cattle but when he had spare feed or thought he could make a quid by buying steers to fatten in the feedlot, he would come to Roma and buy.

Wallace was not only a character but a legend and when he left us in 2007 aged 82 he left a hole in the industry that no one is ever likely to fill. There is no one else like Wallace Logan.

There would be thousands of people that would have known him better than me, but I'm going to write this bit myself as my own tribute to a great cattleman.

I heard about him before I met him. Back in the sixties when I was cutting my teeth as an agent, they told stories about him and the number of bullocks he could fatten on "Warrinalla" north of Injune.

When I was in Richmond I did an inspection with him at "Delta Downs" out from Normanton and when I was in Townsville I ran into him several times.

They were selling 600 "Ucharonidge" Brahman steers from the Territory at Richmond and I went out with four orders to buy the lot. Wallace turned up and blew me out of the water; he got 550 head and I got 50 of the tails at the price I wanted to pay for the tops.

Another time I got off a small plane at Townsville and entered the crowded terminal building at one corner.

Wallace, wearing his trademark khaki shirt and pants, in high heeled boots and high crowned ringer's hat, was in the diagonally opposite corner but was tall enough to spot me over the crowd.

As soon as our eyes met he charged through the throng with hand outstretched and roared: "Don't say you don't know me you bastard, don't say you don't know me!"

What a greeting. Royalty has never been welcomed so warmly.

In the early nineties, my wife Lurelle and I did a trip from Roma that took us up into the Gulf. We called into "Magowra" at Normanton to see Wallace and meet his wife Dorothy and were overwhelmed by their hospitality.

He bought Archer Station at Rockhampton, sold Magowra and moved his headquarters and although he was getting older I think he became more active than ever before.

He'd turn up saleyards and buy all the good quality fattening age steers and neither the price nor the number seemed to bother him. If he wanted them he bought them and some auctioneers may have had a few extra bids on him to push the job along even further.

In 2006 Roma saw a lot of Wallace. He came down half a dozen times buying steers to go into feedlots or to fatten on his Injune and Rolleston properties and as a buyer he was just as unstoppable as he was when I first tangled with him in Richmond 40 years earlier.

But one day on one pen he stopped bidding. Perhaps he thought the auctioneer was having a go at him, perhaps he thought they were dear enough, or perhaps he thought he still held the bid, anyway, doesn't matter, that pen went to Tony McLennan who fattens a lot of steers on oats at Yuleba.

Immediately they were knocked down John Dearden went over and patted Tony on the back saying:

"You'll remember this day all your life and you'll be able to tell your grandkids about the time you outbid Wallace Logan."

Fair comment; he may be the only one who ever outbid him?

Around the saleyards there was conjecture about his age; some said he was 90 while others reckoned he was not much more than 70. I never knew how old he was only that he was a lot older than me, so I asked him.

This is what he said:

"I was born on 22nd June 1924, the second shortest day of the year; I never finished what I had to do that day and I've been trying to catch up ever since."

To my way of thinking, that sums him up. Wallace was always on the go, always doing something … something big!

Barrie Loughnan is a member of the Loughnan clan that has inhabited the Maranoa district for over 100 years. Barrie himself had "Alicker" north of Roma till he moved into town but he still retains an interest in the paddock known as "Bells" where he runs a few cattle.

He was a Bungil Shire Councillor 1975-91, Shire Chairman 1985-91 and a member of the Saleyards Board 1976-91, and he has always sold cattle through the saleyards and continues to do so.

In the last 30 years, Barrie has seen a lot of changes at the yards, in fact in some cases he was instrumental in making them happen. He was on the Board when the scales were installed and the liveweight selling of fats was introduced.

Originally the yards were built to hold Herefords and there was nothing prettier than the sight of 7000 whitefaces packing the yards to capacity, but as bigger crossbred cattle were introduced, something had to be done to keep them from jumping out of the pens.

Before he retired from public life, the first rows of steel selling pens had been constructed partly replacing the timber yards completed in 1969. At that time, the Board was debt free and Barrie's parting advice was: "Borrow a million and keep going!"

History records that is exactly what happened and continues to happen as the yards are expanded, improved and upgraded.

These days, Barrie lives just across the highway from the saleyards and he rarely misses a sale.

"I like to watch out for Loughnan family interests," he says. "They can't always be there to see their cattle sold, but it's no trouble for me to keep an eye on proceedings, to see them weighed and to ring them with the prices.

And I know all the buyers and the agents; I have breakfast with them!"

Barry is the sort of bloke who likes meeting people; he loves a yarn and with his background, who better to explain to a stranger the history of the place and how it all works?

You'll see him each saleday, up on that big platform overlooking the yards, saying g'day to everybody, talking to old mates, chatting with visitors, answering questions and explaining to tourists, who have never been to a cattle sale before, what is really going on … unofficially.

Barrie is an ambassador for Roma Saleyards.

He's been approached to wear a badge and take on the role officially and would have jumped at the chance to do so on a volunteer basis till he found that he had to do a course and be lectured to know what he already knows and to do what he's already doing.

"Not bloody likely! I'll just do it my way."

When you come to Roma Saleyards, look out for Barrie; go up to him and say, "Are you The Ambassador?"

You'll enjoy meeting this real life character and, take it from me, he'll know what's going on!

Cath Cocks, aka "The Queen of the Canteen" aka "Mother Superior", ran the saleyard canteen for 25 years from 1st September 1980 to 18th August 2005. This is her story:

Various volunteer charity groups were trying to cater for the swarms of people attending the sales but it was getting out of hand and the Saleyards Superintendent, Keith Kimlin, approached me to take over the catering service as a business.

When I started there were three sales a fortnight, six weeks off for Christmas and two annual Hereford Bull Sales that attracted huge crowds.

The facilities provided were zilch! There was a hole in the wall so you can imagine the flies and the dust. There was a pine table, a Coca Cola water fridge with no lid, a stove of sorts, 30 cups and an old refrigerator. That was it!

My first day was a Hereford Bull Sale and we were to serve a complimentary afternoon tea to all and sundry. Talk about being thrown in at the deep end!

The charity groups used to serve only corned meat sandwiches but in the first couple of weeks I bought two dozen mugs, hot plates, a couple of toasters and a pie warmer in order to vary the diet and improve the service.

At that time, breakfasts were eaten standing up around the tank stand which was pleasant enough in winter but not so good in summer.

Eventually the front area was closed in, tables and benches were provided, air-conditioning was installed and other improvements were made but at the same time cattle numbers were increasing, more people were coming, and the canteen was getting very busy.

I recall one day in the eighties when the drought was on and we had 10,000 head; we started at 5.00am and finished at 10.00pm by which time tempers were a bit frayed. John Waterworth brought ice and cold drinks from town all day and we served them out of the Coca Cola fridge - we went through 86 dozen of them!

On any given sale day, Val Harms was always one of our first customers. He'd order one strip of bacon with eggs sunny side up then tell us a joke. We would hear the same story several times, perhaps with a bit more added to it, but we would always laugh even if we didn't get the punch line.

I don't know how many jokes I've heard over the years but had I written them all down and produced a book it would have been a bestseller.

As years passed the sales increased to two a week every week except for three weeks off at Christmas, and bull sales got up to 17 a year not counting the special night sale when the auctioneers dressed in dinner suits.

On that occasion we ladies in the canteen felt a bit out of place without our lipstick, ball gowns and stilettos.

At one bull sale two young blokes carrying a jar of coins and a bible bought a bull for $6500. When time came to pay they kept bursting into song praising the Lord and quoting from the bible, but God must have had other ideas because they were about $5950 short when the contents of the bottle were counted.

But I'll let Gary Greer tell you the full story.

Roy and Judy Reynolds from Moorlands Stud were here for another bull sale and Judy came up to the counter and asked,

"And dear, what sort of wine are you serving today?"

My reply was, "Sorry, no wine here today," and she said,

"I just knew I had to bring my own!"

Another day a psychiatric patient escaped from the hospital and walked out to the yards. He came into the canteen, had coffee and sandwiches but didn't pay, went over to the sale for a while, came back and had a steak sandwich but still no money.

Keith Kimlin had a word with him and told him nothing was free and that he would have to pay and, to cut a long story short, Keith ended up ringing the police.

As it turned out they were looking for him and were glad to find out where he was, in the meantime the girls were hiding all the knives and anything sharp.

Des Cherry, the Roma branch manager for Dalgetys, was promoted to a senior position in the Brisbane office but he came out to Roma sales fairly often.

This day he flew out in the morning, arrived at the saleyards, went to the toilet and, bingo, the zip in his pants broke.

He snuck around to the back door of the canteen with his shirt hanging out and his hands covering vital parts. We thought we might be in for a strip show but he was too red in the face for that.

Anyway I got onto Molly from up on the hill and she came down armed with safety pins, needle and thread.

It' easy enough to sew things flat on a table but, let me tell you, it's no easy task pinning and sewing up a zip from the outside with a bloke like Des wriggling around on the inside and it took a bit of doing to stitch him up nice and tight.

I said to him, "If you don't eat or drink too much you won't have to go to the toilet," but late in the afternoon he came back in real discomfort; he was due to fly back and he wasn't going to make the airport let alone Brisbane.

"I've just got to go right now," he said.

So we unstitched and unpinned him; he went, and then I just stitched him up again and wished him all the best.

Another day a young fellow was walking towards the canteen when he collapsed. Therese Munro and I rushed over to him; his pulse was going crazy so we rolled him on his side and called the ambulance. Next thing, he got up and walked off.

The ambos arrived and found Therese and I standing there completely gob smacked with no patient. Later on we were told that sort of thing happened fairly often to the same young man so we didn't feel so bad.

Lyall Coggan was an old bachelor bloke and a regular customer. He always ordered the same meal, would always ask the price and every time Pat Allwood would tell him that it cost $10.50.

And Lyall would say in the slowest of slow drawls, "Ten dollars fifty, crikey, I'll have to sell another bullock to pay for that!"

This day he was leaving the canteen with his back to us heading for the door when his satin boxer shorts fell to his ankles.

"Ooopps!" he said.

There was nothing but bare flesh underneath. What a sight!

Anyway, he turned around front on to see if anyone was looking, but we averted our gaze and pretended nothing had happened.

Before he went to Goondiwindi, Dalgety agent big Paul McCormack lived on his own across the road from me and was a great neighbour.

One evening the phone rang and in a tiny squeaky voice he begged me to go to the chemist and get him something.

I mixed up a brew – one cup of rum, one cup of lemon juice and one cup of honey – and took it over to the patient.

"Here, sip this bit by bit through the night and we'll see how you are in the morning."

He drank the lot, reckoned it was okay and asked for more.

So I made him another batch and he downed that too.

Next morning Big Paul was himself again; he was on top of the world, his voice was back and yelled out across the road,

"Cath, you're the best doctor in town."

There was a chap who used to bring his cattle over from Alice Springs and he always has these two aboriginal drovers with him. I'm sure their names were Eddie and Charlie.

They could only speak pidgin so the boss would come up and say, "Just give them whatever they want and I'll fix you up."

Well we didn't know what they wanted and they couldn't tell us so we would give them a steak sandwich and a can of Coke.

They were such gentlemen; they'd stand back and wait and I'd call them forward, and all they could get out in proper English was,

"Tanku lady, tanku lady." It was a real pleasure to serve them.

The Roma Saleyards steak sandwich became known throughout Australia and in other parts of the world as well.

The rural reporter from the ABC in Toowoomba came out and did an interview about how we cooked the steaks. Next day I heard the story on the radio from Toowoomba and got a bit of a buzz.

Two days later my cousin Peter Howard rang. At that time he was one of the leading chefs in Sydney and he had heard it too.

"How the hell did you get on the ABC," he said. "I've been trying for years and I can't ever get on there!"

Next thing I got a call from somewhere in Victoria. "Yes, now I know how to cook a steak; good on you."

I was at Auckland airport on my way home from Tahiti wandering around among the crowds, killing time, when I heard this fellow saying, "Excuse me", then a bit later "excuse me", but I took no notice and kept on walking.

So he came up quite close to me and whispered, "Steak sandwich, Roma Saleyards!"

Well that made me stop and turn around in a hurry. I recognised the face but couldn't remember his name till he said, "It's Richard."

"Oh, yes; Richard from NSW."

"That's right; I remember you and your steak sandwiches."

Before I left there was this German couple. They had visited Australia for five years running and on this occasion they were heading west.

They came to the saleyards about 7 o'clock, had a look around, went over to the cattle pens, came back to the canteen, had a bite to eat, went to the sale, came back to the canteen again, had a drink, then away they'd go back to the sale ... this went on three or four times.

Anyway, I started up a conversation – they spoke good English – and I asked them what they thought of the saleyards.

"Well," they said, "We have never ever seen anything like this before, and they're all different and there's so many of them."

They were so taken in they kept going back over.

"But," they said, "We can't understand all that garble and noise that the people doing the selling are making; we don't know what they are saying at all."

I told them not to worry because nobody else can either.

I asked, "Do you eat a lot of meat?"

"In Australia we eat meat three times a day; in Germany it's too expensive so we don't eat meat at all."

That day I think we had about nine or ten thousand and I said, "Have you ever seen this many cattle together in one place?"

"Good God girl," she said, "There's not that many cattle in all of Germany!" It was time to hand them over to The Ambassador to complete their education.

My last few years in the canteen were the busiest. We were starting off the day doing 50 breakfasts with "bum nuts" (Dubbo buyer Tony Morcom's name for eggs) sunny side up, rock hard, medium or medium rare, then onto steaks for smoko and lunches. If I had a dollar for every steak I cooked over the years, I'd be a millionaire.

But I have no regrets only happy memories; it was such a great experience to have met so many wonderful people.

Dexter Kruger is the oldest person at Roma saleyards on a regular basis in fact he was still buying and selling cattle when he was 96.

Dexter is one of the Krugers of Sheep Station Creek, Kilcoy, and he has written his own book by that name to record the full story.

He started trading cattle in his own name when he was only 16 and acquired his first block of land while he was still in his twenties.

By 1942 when he was 32 he was a successful dealer and owned more country; he married Gladys Beanland and the couple moved to Kilcoy and started raising a family.

Forty years later the family and the operation had expanded. Dexter and Gladys lived in Nanango and owned "Beverley Hills" while Dexter's son Gregory had grown up, married, had two sons Daryl & Steven, and bought the nearby property "Karnoone".

The powers that be then decided to build the Bjelke Petersen dam which flooded half of Karnoone and the property was resumed. There seemed to be no room for the Krugers so they all moved west.

They bought "Bonanza" south of Roma in 1986, followed by "Waratah" then "Oberina", which adjoined the other two, in 1991.

Dexter and Gladys lived in town, Gregory and the boys on the properties, and Dexter attended every store sale and most fat sales, buying stores or selling fats and keeping in touch with the market.

He may have been new to Roma, but he was no stranger to the saleyard scene. For the previous 60 years he had been buying and or selling at Esk, Toogoolawah, Colinton or Cannon Hill saleyards.

As a saleyard man he was way ahead of his time. In 1951, as a member of the United Graziers Association, Dexter moved the motion to have liveweight scales installed at Cannon Hill.

Twenty five years later in 1976 the scales were installed and the liveweight selling of fat cattle became a reality. Another 25 years went by before liveweight selling of stores was introduced in Roma and Dexter was there on 9th January 2001 to see the first pen sold.

But what of the Krugers in Roma?

Gladys went to God in 1994, Gregory and Steven sold up and moved away, Daryl sold Bonanza in 2006 and put his money into his own earthmoving business, and that left Dexter.

Right up to 2006, while the family still had property and when the season was right or they had surplus grain, Dexter was on hand to buy the stores needed to complement their fattening operation.

This elderly veteran knows about saleyards, he is a saleyards man. He was the oldest active operator buying and selling at Roma Saleyards right up to last year; he could hardly see, he could hardly hear, yet he did the job, did it well and he did it on his own.

Dexter is now 97 but he visits the saleyards when it's not too hot; you'll find him seated on a bench under the Trees of Knowledge.

Sit down, spend time with this character, listen to his stories, ask about his poems; you'll find it a very worthwhile experience!

Terry Garvey first came here in the fifties with his father, the legendary agent Bill Garvey, who was with Goldsbroughs in Miles.

Bill bought a lot of cattle in those days and Terry must have acquired a taste for the job because he became a cattle buyer when he was still a teenager and has never been anything else.

As this book goes to print, he's been buying continuously for 47 years and seldom misses a Roma sale.

These days "Garve" maintains an interest in the industry buying for Stanbroke, and others. It's significant that he retained the order after the change of ownership a couple of years back; obviously the new people value his services as much as the old company did.

You could describe Terry as an upright man, a well respected senior buyer, or at least that's how I see him, and I have no doubt others see him the same way.

He bought for Anderson Meat Company for over 20 years, the only permanent job he ever had, and the rest he bought for on a commission basis and that includes Stanbroke.

To buy for the same people for a long time you must be doing something right and you only have to see Terry in operation to understand why his clients have stuck with him over the years.

But there is another side to this character – his wit!

He is a genuinely funny man with a unique sense of humour and his expressions are priceless. Here are a few examples:

On Queensland State of Origin selection:
There'll be a riot at Aurukun if they drop that Matty Bowen.
On Ricky Stuart's appointment as ARL coach:
Ricky couldn't coach a pig to get dirty.
On the overnight curfew for cattle:
Have these been curlewed properly?
Describing someone's physique:
As fat as a match.
When asked, "How are ya goin?"
Okay from the ankles down.

He's come out with hundreds, no one can remember them all, but if you ever want to hear some of his original quips, just follow the sale and stay within earshot of Garve on any Roma saleday, and you're bound to pick up a gem or two for your trouble.

Jimmy Matthews lives in Melbourne and looks after major corporate clients for Landmark. He is seldom seen in Roma but when he's here something big is on.

He's been at it for a long time and go back 10 or 15 years and he was often described by Stan Wallace in the Country Life as the "guru" of Dalgetys Livestock.

Nothing has changed as far as Jim is concerned; Dalgetys became Wesfarmers then Landmark but Jim just kept on selling cattle only in bigger numbers.

When you see big lines of stores at Roma on account of the likes of Sidney Kidman & Co or Consolidated Pastoral, you can be assured that Jim Matthews had something to do with them being here and sometimes he is here himself.

You'll recognise him instantly. He'll be immaculately dressed in company corporate uniform, trousers pressed, boots polished, tidy shirt and around his neck a matching green scarf.

Jim has had throat cancer. They carved up his neck and took out his voice box and he covers the scars with the scarf.

Once a brilliant auctioneer (who could find a lot more bids than the buyers ever made), Jim can no longer talk and relies on voice transmission with the aid of a Servox that he presses against his throat to communicate.

A lesser man would have packed it in, called it a day, taken retirement and gone fishing but Jim carries on as if nothing has happened. If anything, his circle of influence has been widened throughout rural Australia.

He's a colourful character with a unique turn of phrase and his own sense of humour. This story will give you some idea of the man:

Jim was visiting a large branch in a provincial town somewhere within the Landmark empire when a young man working in the Merchandise Department approached him and asked for advice.

He had long untidy hair and a scruffy sort of beard and he wanted to know what he should do to get into Livestock.

Jim held the machine up to his throat and said, "First of all, smarten yourself up, get a haircut, comb your hair, have a bloody shave, look like an agent instead of a hobo, and when you've done that come back and ask me again."

Note: *Readers should insert a few of their own favourite expletives into the previous sentence to get a true feel for the real tone of the advice!*

The young bloke went away, had a thought about it and came to the conclusion he'd been harassed, so he went to management and told them what naughty Mr Matthews had said.

Management considered that an apology from Mr Matthews was necessary and the sooner the better; they were keen to nip this in the bud before the complaint became more serious.

"You can't speak like that to staff. Tell him you're sorry and let that be the end of it before he lodges something more formal."

So Jim rang the branch and asked for the lad.

"Are you the young fella that asked about a Livestock job?"

"Yes, that's right."

"Very good; now you listen to me. I meant every fuckin' word I said! Go and get a haircut."

You always know where you stand with Jimmy Matthews!

John Bushell came to Roma as a meat buyer for Borthwicks in 1962. Over the next 40 years he was associated with the saleyards as a buyer, a vendor, a butcher and also as a Charolais breeder conducting the best no-nonsense stud sales you have ever seen.

With that background you will realise he has done most things that can be done at the saleyards.

He hasn't been an auctioneer, but he's told plenty of them how to do it, and he hasn't actually managed the place, though he has opinions on that subject too.

But he has bought a lot of cattle, thousands of them, and he's the only commission buyer I know that stays back to check the count, check the loading and make sure everything is right before they leave. Sometimes he's out there most of the night!

And he is still buying and selling, and he attends every store sale on behalf of his many contacts so that most days "Bush" is one of the major buyers.

He didn't just become a buyer, he needed training. If you've ever wondered how he got the way he is, consider his cadetship.

This is his own story of those early years; it explains a lot!

My first job was to chauffeur Borthwicks buyer George Sandall around the western circuit every month.

We'd leave Toowoomba; drive to Cunnamulla then on to the sales at Quilpie and Charleville. On this occasion we stayed there a couple of days to do a few jobs in the paddock. Here George ran into Anderson's buyer Dick Gleeson and the pair got on the booze.

Dick was a heavy drinker, George was only about two shandies behind him and they were both pretty much the worse for wear when Frank McMahon, the boss of Andersons at Wallangarra, rang Gleeson to say they didn't want the 800 "Bulloo Downs" cows that he had bought.

At this stage the cattle had been loaded at Quilpie and were on the train en route to Wallangarra.

After several more hours on the grog, Sandall and Gleeson came to the arrangement that if McMahon didn't want 'em George would take 'em, so I drove them down to Charleville railway station.

The train was there. George squinted through the slats in the K wagons to get an idea of the cows he was buying, then they went to

118

the office and changed the destination from Wallangarra to Murarrie, patted each other on the back and went back to Corones Hotel.

About 10.00am next day George rang the Livestock Manager, Pat Kitchen, to tell him he had bought the cattle and gave him the particulars, the number the description and the weight, all of which he got from Dick Gleeson.

When Pat asked when to expect the cattle, George says:

"If you look out the window you'll see 'em unload!"

Dead silence, so George says, "I'll see ya," and hung up.

The boss of Borthwicks at the time was Mr. Van Homrigh; we called him "van Haemorrhage"! Ten minutes later he was on the phone and there was no room for any misunderstanding:

I was the driver and we were headed for Murarrie.

Well we got back to the plant and George was on the mat for about two hours while I waited outside.

In Van Homrigh's office there was a couch and when things weren't going too good, he would lie down on it, hold his head back and murmur, "Oh dear oh dear," and such like.

Anyway, George eventually came out and I asked him how he went and he replied:

"I had him on the couch boy; I had him on the couch!"

I also trained with another Borthwicks buyer, Bob Bateman. He was extremely loyal and patriotic towards the company.

In those days they had sales at Condamine and we were there this day along with Gordon Menzies from Swifts, Albert Plummer from Tancreds and Harry Davies from Fields.

There was quite a big yarding and these blokes all go out the back of the shed and draw straws to see who is going to buy all the cattle. Bob Bateman won.

The deal was, one was to kick start the bidding, the others would throw in a bid, Bateman would buy that pen, the next, and the next … and when it was over they would split 'em up between them.

Normally, all these guys hated each others guts, but in a situation like this they were absolute buddies.

I was the jackaroo; I was there to shutup and learn. I knew what was on but was told to keep my mouth closed.

After the sale it was my job to go to the little office, check off the prices and sign for the purchase on behalf of Borthwicks. I was doing this when Bateman walked into the room and said to the lady doing the books:

"Under no circumstances are any cattle to be transferred to another meat company." He had bought 'em all as planned; now he refused to split 'em! Well, all hell broke loose!

But Bob Bateman was such a massive powerful man – he had hands on him like hams - no one was game to take him on, and it wouldn't have done any good had they all tried to take him together.

We got all the cattle that day but from then on it was different, very different, and whenever we came up against any of those buyers at a sale it nearly came to blows.

I had settled into Roma and I was to inspect bullocks belonging to Colin and Nancy Carroll. I'd been told that they were good bullocks, to buy them as best I could, but not to come home without them.

I get up there and made an offer fairly close to the asking price. Colin was happy and would have accepted the figure, but not Nancy. So I had another go. Colin was delighted but Nancy shook her head. This went on four times and after an hour of these negotiations I hadn't bought the cattle.

There were turkeys everywhere, 400-500 of them so I told Colin I'd pay their price on the cattle if they threw in a turkey.

He was over the moon but when he told Nancy she said:

"We'll accept his offer for the cattle, that's okay … but he doesn't get the turkey!"

After I left Borthwicks, I established an association with Peter Lord in Dubbo and most years I would handle about 30,000 cattle or him.

He had all these graziers, a remarkable network of clients, and you would send cattle down and he'd split 'em all up in lots to suit them. He always had cattle to sell because he made the effort to have the supply on hand in the first place. He was a master at it.

He'd fly up to Roma a couple of times a year himself just to see what was going on and have a look around, but even when he was here I did the buying. That was my job.

Once a year, Peter Lord, Val Harms and others would go deep-sea fishing off Gladstone. This went on for 20 odd years or more. After 10 years or so, I raised the question about getting a berth.

"No," he said. "You can't come; you've gotta stay home and make sure the cattle keep coming."

Over the years, a lot of funny things happened at the saleyards. This one will always stick in my mind:

Remember Johnny McMahon? Continual yap yap yap like a bloody fox terrier; at it all the time; couldn't shut up; never stopped!

One day he gave a bit of cheek to another buyer, John McNally. Now McNally was just the opposite of McMahon; he was a sombre more serious type of bloke and he'd had a gutful of McMahon so he wheeled around and tried to grab him.

He was that wild he would have killed him. He missed but he did us a favour: there was not another word out of McMahon all day.

Jimmy Coleman was here again last week and I greeted him with:

"Howaryagoin?"

"I'm a bundle of size seven swerves," was the reply.

Jim lives at Dalby and drives out to the sales twice a week. He has been doing that on a regular basis since 1975 and notches up about 100,000km a year.

"You should know the way by now," I said.

"Yeah; but I got lost a few times going home, and one Thursday morning coming out after the Mundine fight on Wednesday night, by mistake I put Aqua-Ear in my eyes to stay awake."

For those unfamiliar with Aqua-Ear, it's about 70% metho!

Up till January 2007 Jim was buying for ten or a dozen different clients every week. These days he is associated with Mort & Co and buys for them more or less exclusively.

His experiences cover plenty of country apart from Roma and involve heaps of blokes and all sorts of unusual situations.

He says they used to fly out to Charleville to do the western circuit when they still had sales out there:

"There were four of us in this plane, plus the pilot, and we were just coming past Wallumbilla when we realised that this bloke didn't know where he was.

He couldn't navigate and was following the road to make sure we got there, which we did, but it would have been a bastard had we run into a bit of cloud.

Anyway, we sacked him as soon as we landed and came home as best we could when the sales were over."

Jim played A Grade Rugby League and he knows a lot of the old players, so it stands to reason that many of his yarns refer to football.

"A beast got out at Dalby and spreadeagled four of the buyers – Reggie Spratt, Ronny Stanton, Colly Williamson and Kevie Sullivan – they've all gone down; all little fellas these blokes, about five foot six or seven, all sort of suitably rounded by middle age, and they're all flat out in the lane.

Ronny Stanton was a pretty fair footballer, he played A Grade for St George in Sydney; anyway he's jumped up' pulled his hat off and said, 'Give me the bloody ball!!'"

Mention any of the other characters like Kevin "Boondi" Healy and he grins and starts again, but they are episodes you have to hear rather than read; you need the background to appreciate the full humour of the yarn.

When you see Jim next ask him about the time Boondi was at home drinking rum and gave "Cootesy" ten in the bin, or why John Galwey drew a big rabbit in chalk on the side of a K wagon of cattle that went down from Roma to Dalby.

He tells the story about Terry Garvey when he was a youthful buyer operating for Andersons at an Oakey sale.

Fred Keong was there and Fred was short of cattle so he was buying everything – bullocks, cows, steers, bulls – didn't matter; Fred was taking the lot, no one could out bid him.

But when the other buyers gave up, Garve hung in there and punted him up on every beast.

They yarded 367 head that day and when they tallied up at the end, Fred Keong had bought 360 head and A.W. Andersons finished up with seven ... and they were about £10 ($20) a head too dear.

Fred goes up to Garve and says:

"Those cattle are too dear for you. Send them in and you'll get the sack; better let me take 'em off your hands."

And that's what happened. Fred finished up with the 367 head and Garve got none ... but he still had a job.

The conversation got around to Wallace Logan.

When I was a young bloke with T.A. Fields in Rockhampton we killed some cattle on weight for Wallace and we've all gone to the local for a few beers as we used to do, and I'm fumblin' around in me pocket looking for enough money to shout a round and Wallace says,

"Have you got any shares boy?"

"Ah, no Mr. Logan, I haven't got any shares."

"Get into shares, boy, get into shares."

I ran into him last year, 2006, and just jokingly I said to him, "How's the shares goin'?"

"Pretty good; I've got $22 million worth. How's yours?"

I just walked away and pretended I had to buy cattle.

"And, Jim, the NRL footy tipping; how do you go in that?"

"No, not in it any more."

"Why not?"

"Well, you know how it is. You make out you are a bit of an authority on the game, you have a bit of a reputation, and you go down the pub for a beer with three out of seven; it's not good."

Jim is a cattle buyer, a professional cattle buyer … and he tells jokes. He is a very good cattle buyer but he's even better at telling jokes, in fact he is the acknowledged No.1 joke teller at Roma Saleyards and you can guarantee he'll have a new one, twice a week, every week … and he is good!

This is one of his:

A young Scottish lad and lassie were sitting on a low stone wall, holding hands and just gazing out over the loch.

For several minutes they sat silently, then finally the girl looked at the boy and said, "A penny for your thoughts, Angus."

"Well, I was thinkin' perhaps it's aboot time for a wee kiss."

The girl blushed, then leaned over and kissed him, and he blushed, then the two turned again to gaze out over the loch.

After a while the girl spoke again, "Another penny for your thoughts, Angus."

"Uh, I was thinkin' maybe it's aboot time for a wee cuddle."

The girl blushed, then leaned over and cuddled him, then he blushed, then the two turned once more to gaze out over the loch.

After a while the girl spoke again, "Another penny for your thoughts, Angus."

"Well, uh, I was thinkin' perhaps it's aboot time you let me poot me hand on your leg."

The girl blushed, then took his hand and put it on her leg.

Then he blushed. Then the two turned once more to gaze out over the loch.

After a while the girl spoke again and said, "Another penny for your thoughts, Angus."

The young man knit his brow. "Well, now," he said, "my thoughts are a bit more serious this time."

"Really?" said the girl in a whisper, filled with excitement.

"Aye," said the lad.

The girl looked away in shyness, began to blush and bit her lip in anticipation of the ultimate request.

And Angus blurted out, "Din'na ye think it's aboot time ye paid me the three pennies you owe me already?"

Footnote: *Since this story was written the new NRL season has kicked off, there are eight teams this year, Jim has come out of retirement to rejoin the tipping competition at the Dalby Leagues Club, and rumour has it he's just not going too badly. All the best "Muscles"!*

Mick Connell came to Roma in 1980 and so he is one of the longest serving agents still working at the saleyards.

He is neither an auctioneer nor a branch manager and he is certainly not a branch clerk or the livestock manager in fact, whenever asked his title, he classes himself simply as "The Worker".

He is a saleyards man and his job is to do all those things that no one else wants to do which means that he's on tap day and night.

This is how he recalls his experiences:

I came from the Riverina, which is in NSW not Victoria, and I soon found out that I wasn't expected to make it in these harsh conditions.

They said: "Don't bother unpacking; that would be a complete waste of time." They said I wouldn't handle the heat or the Fourex beer and that I'd be too soft for a job at Roma Saleyards.

I listened to the advice but as I was already here I decided to give it a go so I put my head down and just kept on working.

Ten branch managers later, sixty or more stock salesmen later, unlimited trainees later, somehow I'm still here and I still turn up for work on Monday mornings.

When I first came to Roma I noticed what rum did to people. It seemed to drastically change a bloke's thinking, and with some of them it changed the shape of their faces, especially their noses.

I made up my mind not to drink Bundaberg Rum but to stick to beer, Fourex beer, quantity didn't matter, and that I would only have a few on days ending in "y" so that would keep things under control.

On Sundays between 5 and 7pm I made it a habit to have one or two with my mates from the Post Office and the Railway and other blokes around town. They are all part of the show you know.

When we used to load the train someone came up and asked how come the train was always early when it was our turn to load.

Well that was because I used to drink with the train drivers.

You see a lot of funny blokes in the saleyards.

"T to T" men, they're the best. T to T - Tuesday to Thursday – they're no good to you on Monday and you can't find 'em on Friday. There's a lot of them around.

The there's the pre-sale blokes and the post-sale blokes. The pre-sale blokes are very important the morning of the sale. They are very neat and tidy, hats on boots clean; after the sale, unheard of.

The post-sale man is hard to find before the sale, hard to distinguish because he's in his work clothes, but after the sale he becomes very important. This breed is very scarce.

It was about half past two on a Friday afternoon at the end of a busy week, I had old clothes on, and the Regional Manager came up to me and said: "Mick, you're not showing much interest in the sale!"

Counting the stores on Tuesday, the fats on Thursday and now the special Stuarts Creek sale on the Friday, there were 20,000 cattle that week and I had been going since the previous Sunday.

I told him he was quite right. Then I added that I had not been to bed for three days, that I had just finished drafting the cows & calves and that at 2.30pm I was going to have breakfast and go home.

These are the things that go on behind the scenes that no one ever realises, but they happen alright.

Calves were disappearing and I was under suspicion.

Unbeknown to me, one of the hierarchy from the Board took it upon himself to hire an undercover policeman to work at the yards, see what he could find out and nab the culprit.

I reckoned something was on but I couldn't work it out till they fronted me in the office.

The Board man introduced the policeman and began by saying there was a problem at the saleyards.

"Yes, I'll say there is. This bloke's out there working for the Board, he's just counted cattle out and he's sent two too many to a buyer at Wandoan. There's a problem alright and he's with you!"

That was the end of that conversation.

One night I got a call to load four decks of bulls to go to Winton. The carrier wasn't expected till the next day and I'd been down the pub for a few, quite a few, so I couldn't drive. Anyway, there was plenty of time so I reckoned I'd walk out to the yards, not very far, about 6km from my place.

I've got the mobile phone in one hand, glasses in the other, all the permits and paperwork, and away I went.

Pleasant evening, cool breeze, poking along, half way there, out on the highway past the motels, roadworks in progress, car coming a bit quick, stepped aside to be sure …

And down I went; there was a drop of about eight feet onto cement! I saw stars and there was plenty of blood. I stood up, shook myself, there was no phone and no glasses but permits still in hand. So away I go again; back up on the road and out to the yards.

The truckie was waiting. He took one look at me and reckoned I must have been in an accident but I assured him I was okay and we started to load the bulls.

Two hours later the job is done and he offered me a lift to town but I had to find my glasses and the phone so I walked again, picked up the lost property and made it home by 4.00am.

By this time the pain was starting to surface and my wife asked me what had happened. I told her she wouldn't believe me and to go back to sleep, which she did

Turned out I had cracked four ribs and split me head open and as you can imagine I wasn't feeling too good next morning.

Four months later I got over that one!

It was part of my job to receive consignments of cattle over the weekend, long distance cattle that come in early to spell a couple of days before the Tuesday sale.

I remember one Saturday when the AACo sent in one of their first big consignments of stores from three places: "South Galway" at Windorah, and "Maneroo" and "Corona" at Longreach.

There were big cattle and little cattle, steers and heifers, some had been treated with HGP some had not, and they had all been carefully drafted and loaded accordingly, pen by pen, 1343 of them.

There were 10 road trains, 40 decks, and it was my job to unload them, keep them separated, then make sure they were properly fed and spelled.

John Fraser was the Branch Manager at Longreach. He did a mighty job. He drew a diagram of every truck and colour coded each pen with the exact details of what was in that pen.

There were seven different drafts. What I had to do was to make sure those out of the yellow pens remained together and kept separate from the other colours, not only coming off the trucks but once they were on the ground, and on the ground they were no longer colour coded so things got a bit hairy.

I refused help; I wanted to be left alone to concentrate on what I was doing, to do it by myself and do it right.

This was our first big consignment of AACo cattle, two of their station managers were coming down to see the sale, we wanted to put on a good show and it was important there were no stuff-ups.

Anyway, to cut a long story short, after the sale on the Tuesday they balanced to the last hoof and no one was more pleased than me.

One vendor sold his Hereford feeder steers privately without an agent and weighed them at the saleyards before the fat sale. The buyer was there to take delivery and rejected 10 head for being too heavy.

Old mate was a bit embarrassed that he now had to come to an agent and pay commission to get him out of trouble.

Anyway we made a spare pen and lined them up in the sale and would you believe it, the buyer who rejected them at 6.30am bought them at 9.15am and paid one cent a kilo more for the privilege!

Back in the early nineties, the heifer job was getting worse and we were last sale. We had a full lane of heifers that no one was going to want, Blake Munro was the manager and he was doing the selling.

I had an order from Broken Hill for a few and I reckoned I wouldn't have a bid till it came our turn to sell.

And just as well I did. When it came to our cattle only two blokes, notorious dealers John Bushell and Kevin Healy, were still operating and they were more or less takin' 'em pen for pen.

So I got in between 'em and pushed 'em along. They still got a few cattle, I finished up with more than we really wanted, but they paid a lot more for their cattle than they bargained for.

The blokes at Broken Hill didn't mind the extra numbers and they were delighted with the quality so we had a win all round.

One Monday afternoon I was coming back from Toowoomba with clients I had taken down to the sale. We had left Roma at 3.00am that morning and I'd had just about enough for one day when the phone rang and they wanted me to go to the yards, the Roma yards.

I could feel something was wrong, I could feel it in me bones.

Anyway, I dropped the passengers off in town, drove back out to the yards, sought out Terry Hyland and he broke the news:

"Shirley Ayers has got cancer."

That floored me; I was broken up and I got pretty emotional.

Shirley and George were both there at the yards, working, getting cattle ready for the Tuesday store sale and I went over and told her to take the day off, not to come to work tomorrow.

"I can't; I've got to work; I've gotta take me mind off it."

That's what she said and she started next morning at 4 o'clock. That's how she handled it right through; she never missed a beat.

As a young wife and the mother of a small child she had plenty to do at home, but she coped with her illness, had all the treatments, and fulfilled her obligations to the company in the office and the saleyards as though nothing was wrong.

The good news is that they got it early and it looks as though she's in the clear. And she's had another baby and that didn't stop her coming to work either. She's incredible!

She is the best workmate I've ever had.

I've been here a while and so too have blokes like Col Brookes, and buyers like Jimmy Coleman and Terry Garvey, all those old buyers that were here when I first came are still here and we're all still mates. That's not a bad effort.

Forty years ago when I was 22 my old boss in Finley told me:

"Being a saleyards man can be a tough life but remember it's also tough on your family. If you get to 25 without making a complete mug of yourself, then you have made a start.

If you make it to 40 and your wife hasn't packed up and left, then you're going alright. If your wife still talks to you when you turn 50 there is hope that you'll make the grade.

If you are still there aged 60 and the wife and kids are still onside, then you are in sight of your goal. And if you make it to 65 with the wife and the kids and grandkids all one big happy family, then you can say you have finally made it as a saleyards man."

Well I'm 63 next year so I haven't got long to go!

Joe Keppel is the manager of Landmark in Wandoan. He has been an agent for 41 years and regularly attends the Roma sales either buying stores for his clients or representing them when they sell here.

"I can remember when Roma was the smallest saleyard on the Western Line. You had saleyards at Quilpie, Charleville and Mitchell; Wallumbilla was the biggest and they got smaller as you went east. But Roma kicked on and got bigger and bigger as the rest shut down."

I asked him how many cattle he would buy at Roma.

"Well sometimes you would go home with nothing; on a big day you'd get 400 and on a real big day you'd get 700.

They all go to my clients; 90% would be to fatten on crop or grain, the other 10% would be backgrounders."

Joe is a big, impressive man who goes about his business without noise or fuss or offence to others; a quietly-spoken, easy-going bloke that everyone looks up to. As he says:

"I've never had any differences whatsoever. I've always got on particularly well with other buyers, opposition agents, auctioneers and people in general. I've never had an argument and I believe if you concentrate on your job you shouldn't have to argue."

Not many agents can boast 41 years in the business. I asked him how long he intended to keep going.

"While ever they're happy to employ me, I'm happy to keep working as an agent. I'll keep going till they say enough's enough and then I might go on as a commission buyer and just keep doing what I'm doing till I decide to retire."

Good on you Joe. We hope you are around for a long time yet!

Bob Harland "Leumeah" Injune has seldom missed a Roma sale for as far back as most people can remember. These days, his mission seems to be to buy anything of value and turn it into a profit mainly through a feedlot.

Twenty years ago he would come down with Don Kelly. There would be a carload of Injune buyers and/or sellers, they would do the sale, have a few at the Queens Arms after the event and Bob, being a non-drinker, was the designated driver to take them all home.

Bob has the cattleman's eye for a bargain and these days you'll find him at the pen where the next bargain is to be found; the auctioneer doesn't have to go looking for him.

Whether it's a single beast painted out, two or three head, or the whole pen, if they are under the rate and suit his specifications, Bob will have a go at them, at a price. He can be relied upon to put a floor in the market.

He doesn't say much and when he does he mumbles so he's hard to understand, but he's a likeable bloke, gets on well with people, everybody knows him and he's part of the furniture at the saleyards.

And if he ever stops coming, he will be missed!

Peter "The Mouse" Holland has been an agent for 41 years. He has worked in 19 towns in Queensland including Beaudesert, Clermont, Bowen, Rockhampton and Dalby. In 1978 he came to Roma.

He's not a very big bloke, just the opposite; when he was younger he was even smaller and the nickname "Mouse" suits him to a tee. But how did he get it?

I was just starting off with Elders in Beaudesert. The local Friday night thug, the king of the town, used to go around putting on blues at dances, picking fights that he knew he could win, and this night he kept annoying me and annoying me till I lost my temper.

I got stuck in and beat him. It's the only fight I've ever won.

Monday morning I walked into the office and Glen Williams the salesman yells, "Here comes Mighty Mouse!" and the name stuck.

That established we got around to talking about Roma Saleyards and about the experiences of its longest-serving active agent who is yet to turn 60. This is his story:

There were a few lessons to learn when I arrived in Roma and I learned one the first night while penning up cattle at the yards.

There was a fellow there by the name of Val Harms. Being a feisty aggressive little bloke I called him "Valerie".

Lightning struck! I very smartly learned to respect Val Harms and I do respect him too; he was a wonderful man. I learned pretty fast that you address people as they are introduced so Val is Val not Valerie and Tom is Tom, not Tommy. It was a good beginning.

You start off thinking you're smarter than the older blokes and you know how to get your cattle into the pens and you pinch someone's yardage up the lane and you think you're pretty good, then all of a sudden you find the gates are shut and your cattle are split in half and you go down to argue with a man who is 20 years older and twice your size and he just looks at you and doesn't answer.

Those sort of things tend to make you realise you're not quite as smart as you thought you were. With my personality I can get upset, and I did get upset, but later on I thought about it and saw the funny side of it and learned from the experience.

There were also lessons to be learned from the catwalk as a young auctioneer taking on fellas like Kevin Healy in his heyday.

Kevin was an aggressive man and you'd try and take a few bids out of him but as soon as you had one bid on Kevin Healy he knew, he knew exactly where that bid came from. He could trim up young auctioneers and make them pay attention.

Then there was Peter Knauer, a no-nonsense man. Peter was a fella who could easily pick a greenhorn. He had to buy at the best price, that was his game; but if you could ever get the respect of Peter Knauer, he's a bloke who would try and help you rather than bring you down. He was never jealous of a younger man having a go.

Actually I rang him one day for advice. I was thinking of leaving the job, moving to another town and starting again.

He suggested that I give that serious consideration. When you change towns and change agents you lose all your connections and have to build a rapport with new people in a new environment and it just may not suit you at all.

I talked it over with Vicky and we decided it was very sound advice and that we would stay put. I realised I was still learning to be a senior agent and the time for a big move was not right.

I did eventually make a change but I stayed in Roma; I left Elders and joined AML&F. Stuart Hutton was the manager and I replaced an auctioneer by the name of Gerry Logan.

Gerry was a gentleman; he was the last of the breed. He would leave the yards before a sale to go home, tidy up and put a tie on.

Along the way AML&F and Australian Estates got together, that happened very soon after I joined, and the next thing you know Elders bought AML*Estates.*

I like to think that John Elliott paid $24m to get me back and picked up the rest of the business for nothing!

But there were too many people in the new conglomerate; there seemed to be a focus on numbers rather than people and while they were sorting all that out I made a move to join Watkins & Co.

I went to Kevin Watkins, offered my services and told him what I thought we could do together to increase his numbers and improve the bottom line.

And we achieved that and it was a wonderful time actually because I was now at the stage where I had reached maturity. I was able to use what I had learned from people like Peter Knauer, Val Harms, Arthur Walmsley, Ron Armstrong and all those senior people.

And I learned a lot from Kevin Watkins too; he was great help.

I was with Watkins & Co up until 1993 when we made the break and went out on our own, Vicky and me, just the two of us, with one little laminated table and two matching chairs.

The first sale we yarded seven head.

Many of the clients that I had serviced stuck with me and it wasn't long before the business kicked away. Then one day I had 1000 head and I thought that was just the greatest thing under the sun.

"The Sparrow", Steve Goodhew, joined us as a salesman and auctioneer. He is just so loyal to me and to Vicky and to his clients. He's still with us; he's like part of the furniture, part of the family so to speak. Everyone likes Steve; he's a good bloke to be with.

But the book is about Roma Saleyards!

It's a vital part of the industry; there is nothing else like it in the world as far as I'm concerned, and the mates you make at the saleyards are your mates till you die.

I've had bad times, serious accidents in cars and in the yards, and the first blokes on your doorstep to lend a helping hand were opposition agents from the yards.

Val Harms was one of them. He was aggressive in opposition, we had our falling-outs, but when things went wrong he was the first one to go to Vicky to make sure she wanted for nothing and that all she had to worry about was me.

I believe I couldn't have made truer friends in any other place; the saleyards create a bond between all those who work there and I'm just so lucky to have been here so long to make so many great mates.

A buyer from Wagga came to me once and asked:

"How can one so small make so much noise and extract so much money from buyers?" Then he went on:

"In spite of the numbers stacked against you, if you maintain your present attitude, you will win, you will be successful."

And Peter Holland, the Mighty Mouse, is still here!

Robert "Rowdy" Rawlins used to work at the yards used to sell at the yards and used to buy at the yards. These days, he seldom sells, seldom buys but seldom misses a sale.

Peter "Pluto" Tudor lives at Gilgandra but has been a regular buyer here since 1961, back in the era when three saleyards were operating.

He buys for a host of southern clients, as well as himself, and not so long back he would buy up to 15,000 stores a year out of Roma.

But Roma's not the only place. Pluto has bought cattle from Melbourne to Cloncurry, and all points in between, and is recognised as a good judge of cattle and a good judge of values.

When the southern season is favorable he's at Roma store sale every week and he's a hard man to beat.

"I like Roma for several reasons," he says. "Dirt saleyards are the only place to buy; concrete is murder - murder on cattle and murder on men. Give me the dirt yards any day.

And you can get decent lines in Roma, big straight lines of good quality cattle, none of this twos and threes business, something you can get stuck into."

He loves a joke, knows all the tricks, and doesn't mind using his wiles to put opposition buyers off their game so that he ends up with the cattle he wants.

Also he has a great vocabulary and a unique turn of phrase. I heard he described one buyer as "a bloke with a dead rat on his lip!"

That one's a mystery to me. You'll have to ask Pluto.

Peter Knauer describes him as "extraordinary".

"There is nobody I know that covers the distances that Pluto does to attend sales. For instance, he would come up from Dubbo, do the sale in Roma, leave there late that afternoon and be back in Dubbo for the sale next morning.

They say he would put a stick under the accelerator to keep himself awake."

"How does that work?"

"I don't know; but he's an extraordinary man who goes to great lengths and travels enormous distances to be on the job.

And he's an expert; he's never wrong."

Pluto can be a real pain in the neck when he wants to be but apart from all that he can be very helpful especially to young blokes starting off and having a go.

At the Ekka in 2006, Tim McNamara ran second in the Queensland Young Auctioneers Competition and earned a trip to the Sydney Royal Easter Show in 2007 to contest the National final.

When he got back to Roma I asked him about Sydney.

"Well I didn't win any prizes but I had a good time. It was a great learning experience and, I must say, Pluto was very helpful."

That's typical of this extraordinary character!

Kevin "Boondi" Healy has been coming to Roma Saleyards for 42 years. He started work with the private agent Knox & Co in Dalby and he would bring a carload of buyers out to the sales back in the days when there were three sets of yards.

Today he would be the biggest buyer at Roma with about 15 orders every store sale accounting for 500-600 a week on average, but on big days he has been known to take up to 1700 head.

The transition from hairy-arsed youth to major cattle buyer didn't happen overnight. I asked him what sort of training he had:

"Driving out to Roma with buyers was the start of it, then I had 2½ years with AML&F Dalby when The Feather ran the show; that was an experience I'll never forget.

After that I was employed by T.A. Fields as their cattle buyer on the Downs and I stayed with them for 15 years.

Then I was an apprentice grazier on 'Macks Creek' and 'Alpha' at Wyandra but never completed the apprenticeship. The cattle market came good so we cashed the places and took the bullion.

By 1984 I was buying for Maurie Morex; I was his only disciple on the Downs but he got big, too big for us, and wanted to be surrounded by professionals so there was a parting of the ways."

Can you imagine how much he learned in those 20 years? Think about the contacts he would have made, the variety of business he did, and the tricks of the trade he would have mastered.

Now fully qualified as an entrepreneur in the cattle industry, an experienced buyer of fats and stores and already established as a fearless dealer, Boondi was able to build a business buying for himself and anyone else who wanted a professional job done.

And that's the bloke you see operating at Roma today, walking up and down the lanes, fooling around, cracking jokes, taking on the auctioneers, buying for 15 different orders, and doing it all on his left ear. Among his other attributes, I suspect he has an amazing memory.

There are lots of stories but he was reluctant to share them with the public through this book but he'd love to tell you on the quiet if you can catch him when he's not too busy.

Like the one about the football banquet at Theodore. John Wittenberg, who played for Australia, was the guest speaker, Jimmy Coleman, Boondi and a few others from Dalby were driving up for it … but they never quite made it; well they did but Boondi didn't!

Anyway, I asked him did he enjoy coming here:

"Mate, this is one of the funniest places you could come to; there's always a bit of life here. But really it's no different to other saleyards – Goondiwindi or Longreach or Blackall – they're all the same.

It's the people! The people make it. No doubt about that!"

With that he took off; it was time for him to walk the lanes before the sale started to see what cattle of the 6000 yarded suited his orders.

After the sale I had a yarn with Jimmy Coleman to get his opinion of Boondi. If anyone knows him well, it's Jim.

They went to school together, played football together, went to the John Wittenberg's banquet together (though Boondi never made it!), both live in Dalby and they often travel to the sales together.

I asked him to sum up Boondi Healy:

I would say without fear of contradiction that he would be the most experienced cattle buyer in the game today, and when I say "experienced" I mean experienced in every facet of the business. The knowledge that he's got would be second to none in this industry.

He's a larrikin, it spills over a bit now and again, but he's good value; you've gotta know the bloke to fully appreciate him.

To give you a bit of an idea, let me tell you about his dog. They were very much alike, Boondi and his dog; they say there is an affinity between dogs and their owners and that's for sure in this case.

Anyway, the dog's name was, a bull terrier cattle dog cross bred by the famous Pluto Tudor. You only had to look at Tambo to see Boondi.

One day after we'd had a few, and because we don't drink and drive, we went home in a taxi.

We pulled up at Mr Healy's abode to drop Kevin off first, Tambo came out to greet us, I waved to Kevin, Kevin waved to me, Kevin waved to the cab driver … and sooled the dog onto the taxi.

Tambo sunk his teeth into the front tyre, the tyre goes … pssshhhhh … I burst out laughing, the taxi driver turns around to me and says: "You think that's funny? That's the third tyre this week!"

Another day we trucked some cattle. It was Friday, all our work was done so we decided to knock off early and have a drink.

We walked in at about a quarter to ten.

The publican was cleaning the glasses and he's got them all stacked up on the bar, Tambo has followed us in, Boondi slapped the counter and ordered two beers for two steers … with that Tambo jumps up on the bar and skittled about six dozen glasses.

The publican does his block, goes right off, and Boondi remarks: "He's a cranky bastard, eh!"

Well, I hope you are able to make something out of all that and
come to at least partly understand a unique character in
Kevin "Boondi" Healy!

Kevin Healy
"Boondi"

Peter Knauer
"The Feather"

Mick Connell
The Worker

Wallace Logan

Pat Clarke

Joe Keppel

Bob Harland

Peter Holland
"Mouse"

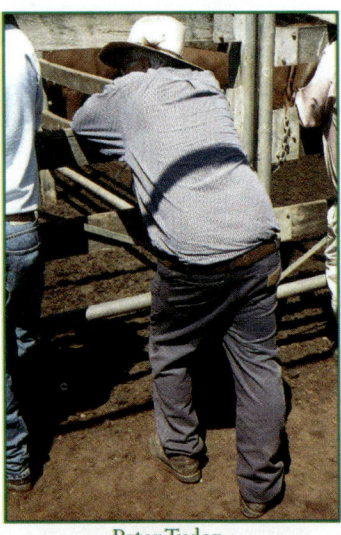

Peter Tudor
"Pluto"

John Bushell
"Bush"

Jimmy Matthews
The Guru

Robert Rawlins
"Rowdy"

Terry Garvey
"Garve"

Cath Cocks
The Queen of the Canteen

Jim Coleman
"Muscles"

Val Harms
"Mr Hereford"

Dexter Kruger

Barrie Loughnan
The Ambassador

Lew Tomlinson

Bryan Hickey

Neville Freeman

Blake Munro

Gary Greer

Garth Hughes

Greg Gibson, East Coast Cattle Co.,
Jericho, with Jason Carswell

Brendan Wade

Gordon Gilmour "Katandra" Dulacca
and Ben Hindmarsh

Marc McKellar with Bob Summerville
"Glenbrook" Charleville

Rod Turner with ABC Rural
Reporter, Alice Plate

Charlie Mills "Tamarang" Wallumbilla
With Mike Connell

Ian Williams "Broadmere" Taroom
and David McPaul

Richard Golden "Potters Flat" Yuleba
with Brendan Raleigh

Peter Holland with
Tony McWhirter "Wilba" Yuleba

Bruce Crichton "Ivanhoe" Morven
and Barry Hughes

Jim Ford "Lewah" Roma
and Duncan McLeod

John Bidgood "Katoomba" Injune
with Don Kelly

Graeme Hubbard "Etona" Morven
with Jason Belz

Jeremy Cahill with
Jason Jeynes "Killarney Park" Tambo

Norm Ehlrich "Greenfields" Wandoan
and Lee Gould

John Rae "Moonambil" Coonamble,
Greg Knaggs & Peter Knaggs
"Eumalga" Dubbo

Rob Irons "Balcondo" Condamine and
Owen Brockhurst with
Cyril Gauld "Bethlee" Drillham

Rob Wildermuth with
Paul Robinson "Alvalea" Roma

Keith Haslop "Wirrina" Dulacca
and Terry Hyland

Brad Neven with
Bernie McFadzen "Farmleigh" Mitchell

Grant, Daniel & Long

Geoff Maslen, Brian Fisher & Jason Belz

P J Holland & Co

Barry Hughes, Peter Holland, Steve
Goodhew & Jeremy Cahill

Watkins & Co

Rex Wells, Brad Neven & Jimmy
Green

Landmark

Rod Turner, Andrew Holt, Brad Vidler, Brad Passfield
& Tony Bowen

Elders

Tim McNamara, Peter McDonald, Terry Hyland,
Dane Pearce & Shirley Ayers

Murray Arthur Agencies

TopX

Andrew Jensen, Cyril Close & Carl
Warren

Ray White Rural

David Murray, Duncan McLeod &
Seamus Filan

Robert Wildermuth & Daven
Vohland

Charlie Cosgrove

Doug Wilson

Detective Sergeant Jim Wilby

Mayors Garvie and Loughnan with
presentation to Tammy Harvey

Nikki Nichol, Gladys Beattie & Libby Tilbury
ready for another busy day in the office

Mandy Golden

Greg Holcroft, Luanne Young &
Philip Edwards of the Livestock Link team

Col Brookes

Stockmen at the scales: Marty Wraight,
Chad McGuinn and Chris Bryen

Administration Officers
Aliesha Waugh, Louise Bain and
Marie Mawn

Trevor Beck

Jim Crane

Canteen Ladies
Susie Kennedy, Eileen Hann,
Louise Bennett & Pat Allwood

Frank McNamara

Natasha Smith

Sharon Wraight & Jack Aspinall

Gordon Johnston

Boosie Crichton
"Myall" Morven

Tom & Margaret Tulley
ex "Springvale" Boulia

Lyle Morton
ex "Roseberth" Birdsville

Cousins Janelle, Tiarna & Pearce Phelps
"Woodburn" Roma and "Warrie" St George

Lloyd & Bobbie Harms "Turramurra" Roma
with Duncan McLeod.

Hazel Krienke

Charlie Clarke
"Eurumbah" Roma

Merle Goodman

The Bench near the Scale House Door.
Spare a thought for the one who suggested it -
Fergus Williams.

Plaques in memory of those killed
in the 1989 plane crash -
Noel Allom, Max McCauley, Bruce Temple,
Wilson Millar and Fernando Rossi –
and of Ross Stewart and Doug Wilson.

On left - the Duke's Gate specially erected in the netting fence pending the Duke's arrival in 2001. Note how foot traffic and drought ruined the lawn.

On right: The Duke's Gate in 2007 - the fence has been lowered, fresh turf has been laid, a new pathway is designed to keep people off the grass, and the memory of the Duke's proposed visit has been preserved.

Kelly, Neale, Zoe & Lindy O'Leary
"Omeo" Injune
enjoy the shade of the Trees of Knowledge.

The five Trees of Knowledge at Roma Saleyards.
Why do we need five?
To accommodate all the knowledgeable people who
come here!

Terry & Rita Jones
Whyalla Stuart SA

Paul Grant & Alan Fraser
Scotland

Narelle Howard & Elizabeth Bryan
Gosford NSW

Roger & Barbara Tapp, Burrum Heads
Jean & David Jones, Sussex, England

Reg & Beryl Gibbs, with Shanti, Murwillumbah
Janet & Angus Davidson, Wales, UK

Lloyd & Kathy Herse
Jacobs Well Qld

Kevin & Marilyn O'Sullivan
North Bondi NSW

Sheryl Shanahan, Freeling, SA
Pam Usher, Chapel Hill, Brisbane

Ken Casperson (artist)
Graceville, Brisbane

Ron & Margaret Lloyd
Albany WA

Robert Knott
Zimbabwe

Monto Landcare Group

Grade 2 & 3 pupils from Miles State School

Signe Eriksen & Morten Petersen
Copenhagen, Denmark

Brian Fisher with Julie & Joe Perry
Cheshire, England

Keith & Lynda Evans
Tennyson, Brisbane

Anne Gilfoyle, Brisbane
with Martina Toggenburg, Switzerland

Elizabeth & Andrew Thompson
Oxford, England
with Daphne Beale, Roma

John & Faye Garwood
Jamberoo NSW

UQ Gatton Campus International students from
Philippines, China, Vietnam, Zambia & Tanzania

EU delegates to World Meat Congress in Brisbane
from France, Spain, England & Belgium with Mayor
Bruce Garvie

Arjan Voorzee & Anneke Postma
Holland

Barry & Helen Smith
Baulkham Hills NSW

Ken & Joan Turnbull
Mt Gambier SA

Steen & Ingrid Dethlefsen
Adelaide SA

Eric Fullbrook
Nabowla, Tasmania

Alan & Mary Carew
Eurack, Victoria

Lincoln & Carla Romero from Brazil with their children Giulia & Laura and Sue & Barry McCabe

Sheila MacDonald (USA), Sheila Dooley (Ireland), Sister Nora Fitzgibbon (Roma), Father John Maher (Roma), Patty Kingston (Ireland), Jan Dooley (Brisbane) & Cath Cocks (Roma)

Gayle & Mark Leonard
Raceview Qld

Steve Gilfoyle with Sarah, Rosie, Joe and Beth from Bald Hills, Brisbane

Helge By
Regina, Canada

8. Agents.

Agents, stock & station agents and woolbrokers, have been on the Australian pastoral scene since the 1840s. They started off as individual entrepreneurs from the "Old Country" bringing out supplies of gunpowder, rum and other necessities to develop the new colony and later acting as woolbrokers, selling wool at auction and exporting to the world.

By the early 1950s Merino wool was worth £1 a pound, or $4.40 a kilo in metric language, the equivalent of about $50/kg in today's money, and woolbroking was the business to be in.

At that time, the rural industry in Queensland was serviced by Australian Estates, Australian Mercantile Land & Finance Co, Dalgetys, Elder Smith & Co, Goldsbrough Mort, Mactaggarts, New Zealand Loan, Queensland Primary Producers Co-operative Association and Winchcombe Carson Limited.

Each of these firms had a State Head Office in Brisbane as well as branches in the bush and it was quite common for the major rural towns like Roma to be serviced by five or six or more of these pastoral houses as well one or two local private agents.

Now we are in the 2000s and the scene has changed. A series of takeovers and mergers has seen those 11 entities reduced to two corporations namely: Landmark, which is the old Dalgety, New Zealand Loan, Winchcombe Carson connection, and Elders which incorporates the rest.

At the same time there has been a rebirth of private agents and franchisees so that Roma still has eight different agents selling at the saleyards every sale, namely: Elders, Grant Daniel & Long, Landmark, Murray Arthur Agencies, P J Holland & Co., Ray White Rural, TopX and Watkins & Co.

While you find ladies in the armed services, working on the roads, playing football, driving forklifts, droving cattle, and they've taken over the banks, there are no female stock agents. Why's that?

There are girls in agents' offices, yes, but you don't see them up on the rail selling cattle and you don't see them buying either?

But, as was stated in the first chapter, this is not a history book nor is it a treatise on the ascendancy of women in the workforce; this is about the people who come to Roma Saleyards, and agents like:

Lew Tomlinson was 19 when he came to Roma as a stock salesman for Australian Estates in 1957. Ardie Slaughter "The Master of the Maranoa" was the manager and Peter Flower was the auctioneer.

Australian Estates had their own yards and conducted regular sales on their own. Lew has some vivid memories of what it was like to be an agent in those days:

There was no bitumen; the road to Injune was the worst track in Queensland and it took two hours to get there. You would go out to do a Charleville sale and you wouldn't think about coming back the same day; it was just too much. And we'd average about eight or ten broken windscreens each a year.

Cattle used to walk into the saleyards, especially for the big weaner sales. A few people would get together to make up a mob and the likes of Les Alexander from "Glen Arden" used to walk in 700 odd of his own weaners.

It may have been 1958 or 1959 when everyone suddenly decided they wanted to use transport and there weren't enough trucks.

Roma Transport had three trailers, no doubles of course all single deckers, Ferg Williams had three, Robby Lister had one, Freddy Wilson had one, Kenny McMullen had one, Don McMillan had two at Surat and George Bromfield kept two at Mitchell.

It was up to us to organise the trucks to bring in 4000 weaners, that's 4000 by transport out of a total of probably 6000. They all agreed to work through the night but it only needed one truck to break down for everything to come apart.

We always sold on a Tuesday. On the Monday we would receive cattle, we'd draft till dark, no lights in those days, I'd spend some of Monday night at the yards receiving cattle off transports, Tuesday we'd be waiting for the sun to come up to start drafting again, then there was the sale, and as soon as the sale was over we'd start on the deliveries.

A lot of the cattle used to go by rail in those days and we would have to walk them to the trucking yards which were down at the Old Surat Road crossing. I always had a horse and Ken Cavanagh and I would take them down in the buyers' lots to put them on the train.

The first train used to load at about eight o'clock, the next train at midnight and the next one at about five o'clock in the morning.

It was a busy couple of days! Then you'd have somebody come along and buy seven or eight hundred, all unweaned, and ask us to tail 'em out for three or four days till his drover turned up. There wasn't much time for sleeping or going to the pub; we were pretty much fully occupied.

One weaner sale it rained, it poured the whole time all the way through; I did the booking up in a plastic bag. The next morning to get to the railway yards we had to walk on the railway line, not the sleepers, the actual rails. The sleepers were covered in water which came right up just below the top of the rails.

Don Henning was another auctioneer who came before I left Roma, Ron McDougall from Wallumbilla would help with the selling and Bob Templeton would come out from Brisbane for the big sales.

Peggy Ashburn and Pat Williams worked in the office and also on the books at the saleyards. Later they both married agents: Peggy married Val Harms and Pat married me.

Buyers came from everywhere.

There were local dealers like Charlie Hassett, Archie Ashburn and Dudley Lalor. Jack Turner and Nipper Bloomfield bought for T.A. Fields properties, and Alan Hepburn was another.

From down the line you had Jack Nugent, Bill Lawton, Dave Kay, Bill Garvey, Jack McLennan, Roy Alexander, Vic Black, Des Archer, Bernie Dillon, Karby Prentice, Ted Bonner, Ken & Warwick Forrester, Larry Diamond, Geoff Fearnside, Don Doro and Len McLennan from Yuleba, the biggest crop fattener in Queensland.

You also had southern store buyers and dealers such as Bob Richardson from Albury, Bill Sylvester, Harry Perram, Roy Keppy, Bill Dickson, Jim Grills, George Manser, Micky Grills, John Cusack, John Carpenter and Tom McMeniman as well as Tim Loneragan, Ted Body from Trangie and Jack Smyth from Tamworth.

When we had a fat sale as many as 20 buyers would be operating including some real characters like Gordon Menzies from Swifts and Freddy Furness from Andersons.

Freddy used to drink a bit and he would say, "I'm into bullocks and beer; bullocks is me business and beer is me fun."

And he would tell stories like the one about the "Millungera" bullocks:

"Big Brahmans they were; you ain't seen anythin' like 'em. We'd walk 'em into the rail at Julia Creek, they'd do 30 mile a day with us holdin' 'em back, they'd truck 18 to the K, heads hangin' out the sides and horns four foot long. Oh, they were big bastards alright!"

And then there was the one about the drover's dogs:
This drover turns up with a pack of savage lookin' mongrel dogs and he's about to tie 'em up when I says,

"I wouldn't tie them dogs up there mate; snakes'll get em!"

But he says, "Snakes don't worry my dogs," and he goes ahead and ties 'em up just where I told 'im not to.

Next morning there were no dogs just pythons wearing collars!

Lester Lehman was a buyer for Borthwicks. The only time I ever saw him stumped for words was at Bill Hartley's, just north of town here.

We were heading up towards Injune to a job and as we went past old Bill's we noticed that he was right up in the top corner drafting cattle on horseback so we reckoned we'd call in on the way back and see what he wanted to sell.

Which we did, and I asked him if he had any steers ready.

He took us up and showed us the cattle he had drafted off. Bill bred beautiful cattle but these were magnificent and at the time Lester had a special order for specific types and these fitted the job perfectly.

But Lester had not met Bill and he wasn't used to his ways.

Bill had one squinty eye and he used to roll a cigarette using two papers so that he finished up with a big fat smoke that he stuck up under his top plate.

So old Bill's rolling a cigarette at the same time sort of looking at Lester out of the corner of his squinty eye and Lester says,

'Well Mr Hartley, how much would you want for 'em?'
'Forty pound!'
'I'll give you forty-five.'
Old Bill keeps on rolling the cigarette and says,
'Listen son; don't tell me how to run my bloody business!'

Lester was a big man and he said that we made a pretty good pair.

He was 6 foot 7½ (202cm) in his socks and I was 5 foot 7¼ (171cms) and he maintained we were the perfect combination to inspect fat bullocks – he'd look at 'em on top and I'd look at 'em underneath and we'd work 'em out between us."

Lew did his first four years as an agent at Roma and
has never regretted the experience.

156

Neville Freeman's great great great uncle, Dugald Carr, was on the jury that tried Captain Starlight, Harry Redford, in the Roma Court House in 1873. From that you will gather that Neville is a local.

At the age of 15, he started work as the office boy with Dalgetys in Roma on 2nd January 1957; Edgar White was the branch manager and Neville describes him as "tough as old boots".

Coming from a sheep background he didn't know much about cattle and approached the saleyards with a whip slung over his shoulder to ward off dangerous beasts, but after knocking other blokes' hats off they took the whip from him, put it in the car and introduced him to a flapper.

As a matter of interest, other aspiring young agents in the same era were Johnny Ashburn who started in the Merchandise at Australian Estates and Cyril Overs who was with New Zealand Loan.

Neville was a natural and soon acquired the knack of shifting cattle, opening gates and drafting then graduated to booking up and taking bids, in fact he always thought of himself as a top bid taker … and still has the knack.

In 1959 he was transferred to Goondiwindi but was back in Roma as a yardman with Dalgetys in '62/63. At that time Robert 'Rowdy' Rawlins and brothers Bob and Bill Isles were also engaged.

"I was on £5 ($10) a day, £6 ($12) if I brought a horse and £6 a night to stay awake to unload the few trucks that came in," he remembers. "I was getting more as a yardman than I was as an agent. It was terrific money. To give you some idea, jackaroos' wages were only a few bob more than that per week!"

For 10 years he was lost to agency. He went shearing in Western Queensland, married Carol in 1967, and then worked for Miscamble Bros Hardware and Building Supplies.

But he was back as an agent in 1973 working at Australian Estates under Peter Flower and subsequently under Doug Kirk, Don Mitchell and Ed Chambers.

He was still there with Ed when Elders joined up with AML Estates back in 1984 but left to buy "Six Mile" at Eumamurrin to accommodate the expanding Charolais and Charbray Studs he had registered in 1973 and 1979 respectively.

Neville also took on the Real Estate work for Richard Foster & Associates, a business that later became Murray Arthur Agencies.

"I was in Real Estate but I didn't miss a sale. I'd be out there meeting people, booking up and taking bids; it was in me blood."

After a diversified career of 21 years as one of those bloody agents, he left to devote all his time to the Charolais and Charbray Studs now located at "Baroola" conducting 18 stud sales through Roma Saleyards up to 2004.

He was on the Bungil Shire Council for 15 years, held the position of Deputy Mayor for six years and Mayor for three, and was a member of the Saleyards Board from 1994 till 2000 when he bowed out of public life.

It's fair to say that Neville Freeman would be the only person ever to be involved in every single aspect of the saleyard operations … except for working the scales and cooking the steaks!

As such, he has a few stories to tell:

In the late fifties we had the big weaner sales, thousands of weaner steers and heifers, and at the end of the day we'd have to truck them, on railway wagons, and the trucking yards were not adjacent to the saleyards as they are now.

So they had to be marshalled into buyers' mobs and walked across to the trucking yards on horseback. Val Harms was in charge of trucking and usually it would be a full train which would load at 11 or 12 o'clock that night.

We would have been up since 3.00am and still loading cattle at 1.00am the next day, so we were pretty weary … and Val Harms wasn't overly tolerant of office boys!

But he knew what he was doing; he really set it all up. He'd yell out, "Right, six K for Billy Lawton," and he'd tell us how many to truck to each wagon, and we'd load them one after the other, then he'd call out, "Now the next 14 K are for Peter Knauer …" and he'd be there checking the counts and running the whole show without missing a beat. It was really good training for us young blokes even if we were half asleep.

The men who worked the sales and camped overnight had little bits of huts to sleep in. When the work was over, one bloke in particular used to get a taxi to bring some grog out.

Norm Harland and Bobby Isles shared this hut and Norm was putting a few away when Bob said to him,

"We haven't finished the job yet, there's a couple more lots of cattle to shift around, so go a bit steady."

Well Norm was a good worker and a good natured bloke but he didn't like being told what to do and when roused he was always threatening to flatten someone. Anyway, he said to Bob,

"If you don't leave me alone, I'll flatten ya!"

Bobby replied, "You couldn't knock the top off a custard tart."

"Listen, let me tell you somethin'; you're gonna see some pretty good punches while your eyesight holds out!"

While I was still the office boy in 1958 the company advertised for a stock salesman. The bloke who got the job was a New Zealander who had been working as an accountant for the Holden car dealer. As you can imagine he was not very experienced.

Anyway he goes into the manager, he's very proud and pleased with himself, and he says, "Mr White, I've just got 200 six-year-old bullocks to sell."

"That's good; whose are they?"

The new man gave a name and the boss scratched his head,

"He doesn't have bullocks; he only sells steers. What did he say? Tell me exactly what he told you."

Turned out he had 200 No.6 steers!

Let me tell you how and why I became a councillor.

When I left Elders back in '84 the mind was pretty sharp after all those years as an agent and suddenly I was a grazier, and the mind was goin' like:

"Well what'll I do now? Go and put a post in the ground ...?"

I wasn't mentally challenged enough doing what I was doing.

In 1985, council elections were coming up, so I nominated and was elected, and re-elected, and I ended up on the Saleyards Board in 1994, and perhaps would have been there earlier had it not been considered that my previous experience may have prejudiced me towards the agents?

Over the years I developed a very good relationship with Garth Hughes, the top stud stock auctioneer of his day and a real man's man.

At Palgrove in 1990, Garth was the auctioneer and I was there to buy a bull. The sale was in progress, there was a problem with the bid, and it looked like they were trying to stick the final bid on me.

Pointing to another bidder as I spoke I said, "It's there!"

Garth said, "Right!" and that was the end of that.

Good connection; we understood each other.

In recent years Blake Munro has done a lot of the selling at our Baroola Stud sales. I'd be up there in the box with him, bit nervous, getting ready to start, and I'd say to him,

"If I take a bid, don't worry about it, I can't help it; it's the agent comin' out in me!"

We spoke for two hours to collate this story, Neville doing the talking while I took notes and taped what he said, and in the end he finished with this line:

"It's the people that make the saleyards; it's the people that run the yards that make it the biggest cattle selling centre in Australia. The people; never forget that!"

And you're right, Neville; that's the theme of this book!

Stan "Old Son" Wallace was transferred from Cannon Hill to Roma in 1958 as manager and resident auctioneer for New Zealand Loan. This pleased him, as after having commenced his career in Charleville and after several years in the Brisbane Valley, he was returning west.

Stan reminisces about those days:

I took over the reins from the well respected agent Arnold Newitt and was lucky to have Bob Gillespie as livestock manager. During that time Bob married a local girl, the delightful Judith Henderson.

After Bob's transfer, Bill Ford was my livestock manager.

Tragically, Bob was murdered many years later when we were both working in Brisbane. He was trucking buffalo out of Darwin when he was shot by a deranged ringer.

In those days there were three sets of yards: the Australian Estates yards, Primaries yards and the "Blue Yards" built by dynamic private agent Dick Condon. Dalgetys and New Zealand Loan each held a one third interest in the Blue Yards.

Val Harms was on Condon's payroll when Winchcombes bought Dick's business and his third share of the yards.

Australian Estates was managed by the famed Ardie Slaughter, Don Henning was the auctioneer and their Wallumbilla manager, Ron

McDougall, also took an important role. The Primaries manager was George Henderson, a gun auctioneer.

Dalgetys was managed by Edgar White who was followed by John Roberts; Roy Huddlestone was their auctioneer.

We all sold on different days of the month. Often over a beer or three at the School of Arts or Eddie Dalton's Grand hotel, George Henderson would float the idea of one set of yards and all selling on the same day, but that was a long way off.

Times change! When George would go on holidays I would man the Primaries catwalk and sell his cattle and he would do the same for me. Our business dealings in those days were either old-fashioned or very honourable as we didn't use these opportunities to try to pinch each others clients.

George had a great staff with Alan Bodman, Fergie Johnson, Doug Heelan and at one time Bill Cooper.

George was on holidays and I was doing the job on his behalf. He had told me about Bill's desire to auction and suggested that I let him sell the bulls. Well Bill did a sterling job and sold a couple of lanes and went on to become an auctioneer of note.

While we had our set clients, dealers were also the name of the game and part and parcel of the saleyard scene. From the southern states we had Claude Sylvester, Jack Smyth, Pat Clarke, and the Richardson brothers to name a few of them who bought cattle from Roma and moved them south.

But we also had our own dealers, such as Carl Waugh, Dudley Lalor, Archie Ashburn and many of our clients who would have a punt with cattle from other saleyards or out of the paddock. Sometimes they won, sometimes they lost, but it all added colour and excitement to the cattle scene.

After the sales were over, and remember we didn't have scales to worry about so we didn't have to wait for cattle to be weighed, we would adjourn for refreshments and as often as not it would be with our opposition agents, their clients and our clients all in together.

They were good days, everyone got on well with each other, we worked hard but we shared plenty of laughs. It might not have been Utopia, but it certainly made for a great life and we wouldn't have swapped it for quids.

Arthur Walmsley was an agent for 46 years of continuous service with one company 1951-97. He took over from George Henderson at Primaries in Roma in 1966 and managed the branch till 1980.

When he arrived there were three sets of yards and sales about every three months. During his time the new yards were built, sales became monthly, then fortnightly, then weekly, and then twice weekly as they are today.

Arthur never held an auctioneers licence but was fortunate to have the services of the likes of John Higgins, Norm East and Ross Kane in that role.

He says he enjoyed his 14 years in Roma, didn't want to leave, but took a job as a Finance Officer with Primac to enable his children to complete their secondary education in Brisbane.

In 1983 he was appointed Queensland Manager of the Primac Property and Real Estate department, a position he held till 1997.

Ed Chambers managed an office in Roma during a hectic period for all agencies from 1979 to 1987.

He took over from Don Mitchell as the manager of Australian Estates but that company joined forces with AML&F and became AML*Estates*. Ed retained the management role.

Not long after that his son, Geoff, rang to ask for advice. He had been offered a position with Elders and wanted his dad's opinion.

"You do what you think is best for you," said Ed, "but as for me, I wouldn't work for the bastards."

Geoff went ahead and took the job and when AML*Estates* became EldersAML*Estates* shortly afterwards, he was quickly on the blower to his father to say:

"Welcome to the company, Dad; but remember I was in first!"

History records that Ed ran a highly successful business for the united operation in Roma before transferring to Rockhampton and into Stud Stock. Twenty years later, as this book goes to print, he is still happily working for the same bastards and he had this to say about his time in Roma:

"My job as the manager was made easy by the calibre of the men who supported me; it was an honour and a privilege to work with them.

There was Merv Fazeldean, who was a great auctioneer, and astute cattlemen like Bryan Hickey and Darryl Harland.

Then there was Mick Connell, Brendan Wade and Peter "Mighty Mouse" Holland.

Peter came to us through the AML&F merger and when Elders bought the business Peter reckoned it was because John Elliott wanted to acquire his services … at any price!

The saleyards really kicked on in the eighties. People throughout southern Queensland and down into NSW would get out of bed on Tuesday mornings and head for Roma Saleyards.

Buyers like Peter Knauer, Pat Clarke, John Bushell and Ian "Slug" Dunstan would not be anywhere else than Roma on a Tuesday.

That was where the action was, the industry event of the week, and if you compare the numbers in the eighties with the numbers in the seventies you'll find there was an 80% increase.

And I wouldn't like anyone to forget that all this was made possible by the people on the ground.

We were all in it, from the manager to the office boy. We'd work at night to draft the cattle, pen them up ready for the sale, and then go home to tidy up so as to look fresh and smart in the morning.

It was a good time to be alive; there was a lot of camaraderie. We all got on well and we'd end up at the Club Hotel after the sale to quench thirsts, tell lies and enjoy each others company and you could bet blokes like Boondi Healy and John Bushell would be there too.

I have nothing but fond memories of my time in Roma."

Darryl Harland has done just about everything around the saleyards except operate the computer in the office.

He's worked in the yards, he's been an agent and an auctioneer, he has bought cattle to fatten on his own property and sold them back through the saleyards, and he has bought cattle for processors and for the butcher at Quilpie. He knows his way around.

Here are some of his reminiscences going back to 1973 when he started with Bert Shaw, the well respected private agent in Injune:

Bert merged his business with Winchcombes so I worked for Val Harms for a short time, then came the cattle slump and I went back home for a while before joining Australian Estates in 1976.

One of my first jobs was to take a buyer out to Peter Sorensen "Junedale" Injune. John Whip came up from Roma and brought Frank Arnold, who owned Arnold Shoe Stores.

Peter had this double of cows, Hereford cows, 40 in the mob, pretty good cows too, and he had $25 on them.

Anyway, we haggled and argued there for about half an hour; all Frank wanted to pay was $23, which was $2/head difference.

After a while Frank said to me, "What are we arguing about?"

And I worked it out for him that 40 head by $2 was $80.

"Well that's only four pairs of shoes; give him his money."

I'd come down from Injune on Monday nights and help draft. Doug Kirk was the manager, and there was John Whip and Doug Thomson.

We'd finish late, long after the pubs shut, but Doug Thomson had a key to the Empire and we'd go down there and have a couple of beers no matter what time of the night it was.

I learned a lot from Bert Shaw and Val Harms, but my real education as an agent started when I worked with Doug Thomson.

We had a line of Murray Cameron's Hereford feeder steers from "Quibet". There were about six or eight pens of them. Doug was doing the selling, knocking 'em down, and I was booking up.

We got down off the rail and he says to me: "I'll have to go and sell those bastards now."

"What do you mean?"

"I didn't have any buyers; none of them are sold yet."

No one picked it; I was standing beside him and I didn't pick it either. He was very good. Needless to say he sold them all in no time.

I'll always remember one inspection that first year. Ken Tomkins had "Westgrove" and "South Westgrove" and ran a lot of breeders and Wallace Logan was to have a look at his steers.

Doug Kirk and Doug Thomson brought Ken Tomkins and John Galwey up from Roma and I took Wallace out from Injune. Put that lot together and you can imagine that I didn't get one word in!

There's 1100 steers he's looking at and we get out there and the cattle are all in the square and the horses are tied up.

Wallace got out, walked over, got on a horse, rode through the mob, turned round and came back, got off, walked over to Ken Tomkins and said:

"I'll give you $50 a head for the pick of 1000 and you deliver them to Boxvale."

That was the deal and we went back to town.

Delivery was the following week. The Westgrove men walked them across to Boxvale. I went out there; Wallace was already there with his wife Dorothy and one jackaroo to take these 1000 steers from Boxvale to Warrinalla.

We counted the steers. Sure enough there was 1000 head so Wallace walked over to the tree where his swag was on the ground, undone the strap, kicked the swag open, pulled out his cheque book and wrote a cheque for $50,000.

That was the biggest cheque I'd ever seen.

Handing it to me he said: "Now Young Harland (he always called me Young Harland) you go straight back to town with that and don't turn left or right!"

I hadn't seen Wallace for a long time but even when he came back to the yards here last year he walked up to me and said:

"Howya goin' Young Harland?"

Another time I brought our client Tommy Warrian down to Roma for a sale. It was a bitterly cold day and I was looking forward to getting home early but Tom had a good sale with his Herefords and he suggested we stop at the pub for a rum.

Well one thing led to another and it was just on dark before we left Roma and headed back to Injune. I was thinking I'd be in trouble by the time I got home but worse was to come.

We were coming up to the Taroom turnoff when Tom announced he would like to check up on a bore. He owned a block up the Taroom road and he had recently done some repairs to the mill and he wanted to see if it was still working.

Anything for a client! Away we go and we get there and we find there is a bit of a noise up the top and Tom says:

"I want you to slip up there; I think she needs oiling again."

So we turn the mill off. It's a 30 foot tower and I clamber up the ladder. I've got me white moleskins on, the wind is howling, and I'm up there swaying around, more from the rum than the breeze, and trying to pour oil where it's supposed to go but it's flying everywhere.

You orta seen me when I got down?

I was covered in oil, grease and bird shit and when I eventually got home stinking of rum I was not the least bit popular!

The things you do as an agent to keep your client happy! But it was a great life and I think we lived through the best times. We were lucky! I don't think there is as much fun in the job these days.

In 1979 we moved into Roma and arrived there the same time as Eddie Chambers who was the manager; I had an auctioneer's licence by then but I was just learning. Merv Fazeldean was the auctioneer.

Another event that sticks in my mind was a big week in 1983. It was the merged company now, Elders AML Estates, and in a yarding of 10,000 we had 6,000 – that would be like having 20,000 in these yards today – and we had cattle everywhere.

We started drafting at 11 o'clock Monday morning and we knocked off at 1.00am on Tuesday. We went home, had a shower and a feed and came back at 2.30am and started again. We penned the last of the cows & calves at 6.00pm on Tuesday night.

I bought some Alice Downs bullocks that day and paid $170 for them. They were four and five year old bullocks, about 100 of them, got 'em home and fattened them by the end of winter and sold them to T A Fields. Noel Toomey bought 'em.

Got a beer and a bottle of rum out of that deal … plus a bit!

Another thing I remember about that sale was a line of 169 cows & calves up round the draft; we sold 'em in one hit and they made $170 a unit, one dollar more than the number.

On Wednesday we had 1000 of our own cattle to get ready for Thursday and by Friday I was footsore and chaffed in the arse. I was deadset buggered; but you were happy doing those things and you felt proud of the achievement.

A bit later on I left the agency to spend more time at home and I ended up buying for Warwick Bacon full time mainly through the connection with old mate Doug Thomson who by then was their Livestock Manager.

In those days, and I'm talking 1989 through into the nineties, we would buy a lot of cattle out of Roma. Most people still had Herefords, which Warwick preferred, and their buying instructions were simply, "Buy the best cattle!" which made my job easy.

Then they started to feed their own cattle so I got into buying quality feeder steers for them, and I also bought cattle for other people down south, and while the drought's been on I've been buying a few for Nev McConnell the Quilpie butcher. He says to me:

"See if you can get us another dozen good little bullocks. There are no fat cattle out here and I can't even buy a leg of mutton."

That's been going on for five years but their season has turned around now and they'll have plenty of their own fats very soon.

Young Harland is a grandfather now. He's the type of bloke that people look up to; he's done it all on both sides of the catwalk so to speak, he's a good judge of cattle, he was a top auctioneer, he only ever buys the best, and although he doesn't say too much, what he says is worth listening to.

Murray Arthur was with Dalgetys up till 1989 when he left to form the livestock side of Richard Foster & Associates. Two years later he bought the operation and it became Murray Arthur Agencies.

By the mid nineties the business had grown to the stage that he needed to bring in a partner, Duncan McLeod, who bought the whole show in 2005 but who still trades as Murray Arthur Agencies.

Talking about his agency experiences, Murray recalls:

"Things would be a bit dead, the buyers getting a bit bored and you'd be half way through selling a pen of cattle, when someone would let off a firecracker to liven things up."

I asked him who would do such a thing.

"Well you can't buy fireworks in Queensland so they have to come from across the border. I don't want to mention names and don't blame Pluto Tudor, but it could have been someone who is very closely related to him."

I presume that would be David Tudor, aka "Pluto Pup"!
"A chap at Injune booked in two decks of cattle with us.

It would seem that he thought that I looked a bit like the then manager of Dalgetys, Mick Browne; anyway the two decks of steers were consigned to me.

It was in the dark when they came in and were penned and I had a bit of a chuckle to myself as I passed old Val Harms in the lane because I knew the client normally dealt with him.

Next morning all hell broke loose with Val up and down the lanes searching for the cattle and he let everyone know about it too.

Eventually he spotted them, sitting up all nice and neat in my lineup. I can tell you he was not amused, in fact he went berserk poor old fella and a very heated argument followed.

Guess what happened? The cattle were confiscated and Val sold 'em! It wasn't funny at the time but later on we laughed about it.

It was all really a mix-up; there was no malice. The bloke who booked them in was a staunch Val Harms and Dalgety client who somehow confused me with Mick Browne."

Gary Greer has been an agent all his working life and although never actually stationed in Roma he has been here plenty of times as an auctioneer at stud sales.

His most memorable experience dates back to the Roma Hereford Bull Show and Sale on 28th September 1990.

This is his story:

It was a hot day. I was doing the selling assisted by trainee auctioneer Peter Daniels and the sale started off the same as the previous 40 sales we had already done that season.

There was a capacity crowd in attendance and a top price of $6500 was achieved in the first six lots.

By mid afternoon the heat, combined with the aftermath of the previous night's activities, was having a sleepy effect on buyers but clearance was at 95% and the sale was averaging an excellent $3400.

We had six lots to go. All I could think about was a cold, rewarding ale to celebrate another successful sale.

Peter was selling and doing a great job, in spite of the pontoon and partying the night before, as he came to the champion bull of the day, Glen Wilga Impulse, owned by Charlie Jones from Chinchilla.

Bidding commenced at $1000 and, under strong competition from two young men in the top row of the stand, quickly jumped to $6500, equal top price. That woke the sleepyheads and created a buzz of excitement in the crowd … but there was more to come!

"Buyer's name please," says Peter.

"The Lord Jesus Christ," came the reply.

Our bookkeeper Bryan Hickey took command of the situation.

"Could I have the buyer's correct name please?"

"The Lord Jesus Christ."

I had never seen Bryan become agitated at a bull sale before but that really set him off.

"Look, it's been a bloody long day and I don't need this idiot reply; all I want is the buyer's name to complete the records."

"The Lord Jesus Christ," said the two young men in unison.

We weren't getting anywhere so I told Peter to get on with the selling and told Hick to leave it at that and I would sort it out with the two young blokes as soon as the sale was over.

Turned out the buyers were two brothers from Theodore but when I took them around to the back of the stand in private I was more than taken aback to find they insisted on booking up their purchase to the Lord Jesus Christ.

I had never struck anything like this before!

They had a bible from which they freely recited passages of how the Good Lord provides his followers with milk and honey, which got on my nerves a bit, and after 30 minutes of listening to their bible quotations, religious chants and singing hymns, I rang the police.

While we were waiting for the law, the pair produced a small jar of gold coins, supposedly containing sufficient cash to pay for the bull. Cath Cocks at the canteen estimated it contained about $400.

When I suggested we count the money the boys said that anyone who opened the bottle would be held responsible if it was found to contain insufficient funds as they knew the Good Lord had provided the full gold payment.

The sun was setting and all my patience had evaporated.

Two detectives arrived. They decided to split the bull buyers and question them individually so as to ascertain what they were really up to.

More bible quotes, more psalms, much chanting, talk of gold from heaven, and an hour later we were no further advanced.

The police decided it was time to count the money even though the young bible bashers maintained,

"If the correct money is not there you will be responsible."

It took a while for the three agents and two detectives to count the $1 and $2 coins but eventually we arrived at the figure of $550 which was $5950 short.

Much discussion followed - more questions, more hymn singing, the bible got another run – it was getting out of hand.

The sale had finished five hours ago, we hadn't had a beer, the detectives had been on the job for over two hours with no progress, and there seemed to be no end in sight.

The father of the boys was at the saleyards and on a couple of occasions he had offered to pay the full price of the bull. The brothers had refused to accept his offer saying that they had purchased the bull on behalf of the Lord Jesus Christ who was the rightful owner and he would provide the gold.

This was not funny! Another hour went by with singing and bible quotations and no sign of a break though.

By now the detectives were very frustrated and could see no way of resolving the matter so I decided to approach the father; that is the father of the boys.

He was just as upset as I was but he agreed to have the bull transferred to his name and his agent agreed to accept the account so we were able to finalise the sale at 9.00pm.

"We wanted to see if the Lord would deliver, and he did," commented the brothers and, faith intact, they drove off in their van.

And Peter and I were left there wondering what else could possibly befall us for the rest of the bull selling season.

Blake Munro started at Roma as a junior with Primaries. It was his first posting out of Brisbane and the start of a distinguished career.

Arthur Walmsley was the manager and Harry Siggs, who was very particular about all things but especially the company Falcon utility, was the merchandise man.

This day, Blake and Bryan Hickey were at the yards in the merchandise ute taking hay to feed cattle. Blake was driving and he successfully negotiated the lane and the double steel gates without scratching the paint work.

They unloaded the hay and Blake was backing out when he drove over the gate stopper - a lump of railway line set in concrete – tore a hole in the sump of Siggsy's precious ute and dropped a gallon of oil onto the landscape.

Mild panic set in. "What are we going to tell the boss; what'll we tell Harry?" says Blake who was a bit shaken by the experience.

"Never mind the 'we'", says Bryan. "You did it, you tell 'em, but I'll say this, they won't like it!"

Well they gave him a serve, a real blast, but he survived the ordeal and went on to become a real identity in the agency business.

Blake recalls those days:

"Liveweight selling had not been introduced at all, cattle were still sold dollars per head and we operated without all the benefits of modern technology … apart from adding machines.

But it was a great time to cut your teeth and rub shoulders with gun auctioneers like Doug Thomson and Stormy Normy East and buyers such as Peter Knauer, Doug Heelan and Wally Humphris.

There was another bloke, Malcolm Kinman, who spent a bit of time with us at the yards. He was about the same age as me but he could ride and he used to ride trackwork for Arthur Walmsley.

In 1987 I came back to Roma to take over from Ed Chambers at EldersAML*Estates* when Ed went into Stud Stock at Rockhampton.

Times were changing. Scales had been built, the liveweight selling of fats had been introduced and during the seven years that I was there this time, the Board started to rebuild the yards in steel.

You think back about those days and the people you worked with. John Moore was a very good auctioneer, so too Brendan Wade, then there was Colin Paix and David NcNally.

Johnny McMahon was a regular buyer, a big buyer, but he was also a bit of a tease and he delighted in winding up young auctioneers.

Well it got too much for McNally one day and he jumped down off the catwalk ready to flatten McMahon in the lane but Boondi Healy stepped in and held him back till he settled down.

Boondi was a bit of a stirrer too but he saved the day on that occasion and I give him full credit for that.

And of course Mick Connell! He was there when I arrived, he was there when I left, and he's still there. He was the backbone of our saleyard operation and Mick knew all the ways to work smarter not harder. He's a legend.

In the end I was a bit sad to leave but in my present role as Stud Stock Manager for Queensland I've been back to Roma several times a year every year and it's always good to be back.

And I can't help but notice the ongoing improvements and expansion at the saleyards and I often think back to the early seventies and wonder how we ever did business in the old facilities

I still have friends in the district and it's always good to come back and do business with old mates like Ian Galloway, Boyd Harms, Alastair Bassingthwaighte, Neville Freeman and John Galwey.

Roma is a bit like a second home to me and I'm looking forward to the next trip out there.

Garth Hughes is not just an auctioneer, he's a specialist auctioneer, a Stud Stock auctioneer, and he's been coming to Roma to ply his trade since 1964.

Talk about the gun auctioneers in the stud business and two names invariably head the list, Dave Watkins and Garth Hughes. Dave has retired, so it could be said that Garth is the No.1 man today.

He is getting on a bit, next birthday he'll be 69. You would expect the mantle to have passed to a younger man by now, but none of the current batch can match Garth's diction, humour and enthusiasm … nor can they outlast him at the bar!

He was blessed with a voice the equal of John Laws and an attitude that could have inspired Frank Sinatra's "I Did It My Way".

His style has not always pleased the powers that be, that's why he was dropped from the Magic Millions team, but I was there that day as a bid-spotter among the crowd of 4,000 and can assure you that every one of them lamented his absence from the selling box.

Stud sales in Roma can get a bit boring, but not when Garth Hughes is selling. If the going is tough about mid afternoon on a hot day and the crowd starts to nod off, bring on Garth, and the scene changes instantly; he has that unique ability to resurrect dead buyers.

These days he resides at Tugun and enjoys the surf. He does not work fulltime only when required to do an auction, but that is practically a daily occurrence during the season August to November.

"I still enjoy the sales circuit; I've made a lot of friends in the bush over the years, none of us are getting any younger, and this is a great way to keep in touch with them."

Brendan Wade was 20 when he first came to Roma as a clerk with Elders under Bernie Coonan in 1980:

Bernie was a bit fiery. He'd had a row with the previous clerk who left in a hurry and I was transferred from Toowoomba to take his place.

Bernie was the auctioneer, Peter Queitzsch was the salesman auctioneer and I did the booking up.

In those days we didn't have any outside help; we drafted all our own cattle so I spent quite a bit of time at the saleyards especially on Mondays and Tuesdays. It was a great learning experience.

I came back to Roma in 1985 as salesman auctioneer under Ed Chambers; he would be one of the nicest blokes I ever worked for.

Eddie was someone you did your best for, not because he pushed you, but because you wanted to do well for him. He had very good management skills, he knew how to get the best out of people; everyone liked him and everyone admired him.

He was too nice a bloke to be an agent!

Anyway, I was promoted to Mitchell as the manager and that gave me a look at Roma from a different angle - we sent in a lot of cattle, mostly stores, mostly Herefords, good cattle from up the river.

Roma Saleyards was big business; everyone sold their cattle through the saleyards, it was the focal point of the store cattle market, the cattle were very good quality, and Roma was the place to sell 'em.

Next thing I was back there as Livestock Manager and auctioneer. We had Johnny Martyn and Doug Wilson doing our drafting, Roma had established itself as the major selling centre, and that was a lot of fun.

Then in 1993 Kevin Watkins decided to retire and Watkins & Co. came up for sale. Kevin rang me up to see if I was interested in buying a share. I told him I was but I had no money.

You know what he did? He guaranteed my loan at the bank! He virtually got the bank to advance me the money so that I could pay him on the understanding that if I defaulted he would pay them back.

That's the class of the bloke he was; he went out of his way to give a younger man a go and I finished up in a partnership that owned Watkins & Co and I became the manager of the business.

We were in a rip-roaring drought. The first sale we had we sold 1000 head at an average price of $178.

When it was over I went home. I was sunburned, I had a chaffed butt from drafting, and I sat down on the bed and cried, and I said to myself, "What the hell are you doing this for?"

But the rain came, the cattle market kicked and I've never looked back ever since.

These days Brendan is the State Livestock Manager for Landmark. He is based in Brisbane but is often seen in Roma.

I asked him, "I suppose we could expect to see you out here for the stud sales and special sales?"

"Mate, I think there's a special sale in Roma every Tuesday.

The buyers are there, the cattle are there, everybody's there every Tuesday. It's the focal point, the event of the week. Roma's special every Tuesday and that's what people should remember."

Don Kelly came down to Rolleston from North Queensland in 1983. It was one of those dry years and big numbers of stores were going through Roma. Don decided to come down and have a look.

"I couldn't comprehend ten or twelve thousand cattle all in one yard at the same time," he says, "but they were here alright and that opened my eyes to the value of Roma Saleyards to the industry."

Don's next posting was to Injune and he became more actively involved as his clients were either buying or selling at Roma weekly.

"We had a few active dealers; Bob Harland was one, Neil Stevenson was another. They would buy cattle in The North, bring them down to Injune and hold them in the clean country for the compulsory 28 days, then stand them up in Roma hoping to snag a wealthy buyer from south of the border," he recalls.

"Cattle breeders around Injune would market their weaner turnoff through Roma where they commanded a premium. Coming off light sandy country, the cattle responded very well on better feed and we had some excellent results.

In those days it wasn't uncommon for us to have two carloads at a Roma store sale and as often as not we would celebrate at the Queens Arms before we headed for home.

'Stirling' was half way back to Injune and licenced at the time so on a real good day we would pull in there as well. A day out at the Roma sale was the highlight of the week."

When Don went to Taroom we saw less of him at Roma but he did come back fairly regularly with a mixture of buyers and sellers, probably more buyers than sellers, buying quality steers to take back to finish on the good Dawson River fattening country.

In January 2000 Don came to Roma to manage the Elders branch. No longer was he a visiting agent but part of the action.

"The first thing I noticed," says Don, "is that it's a lot different working here than travelling here for the day."

"The action here goes on and on and on and it becomes a big part of your life. It's a round-the-clock operation; only those who have worked here would realise the hours you spend at the saleyards.

I was here for four years. The first year I made the comment it took a good game to keep me awake till half time watching Friday Night Football; as we got along a bit it took a bloody good game to get me to the kickoff.

Anyway, that's the way Roma Saleyards affects you by the time Friday night comes around; you know you have done your week.

We had a high turnover of staff, particularly livestock staff; not everyone will cop it. We seemed to have plenty of send-offs and welcomes; I lost count. People were coming and going all the time.

Mick Connell was the mainstay of the operation; he's just legendry in my opinion. He's been here a long time, nothing seems to worry him, anything that happens he's seen before, and it's pretty handy to have a man like that in your team.

George and Shirley Ayers were always here; they were our main yard staff. They were certainly a big help to me as they were to all our staff at Roma."

For the past three years, Don and his wife, Christie, have run their own show at Injune, the Elders livestock franchise for that area.

"We still come to Roma," says Don. "This is the main outlet for all our cattle, fats and stores. And we still buy a few out of Roma; if it ever rains again we'll buy and sell a few more!

But times have changed.

After the sale, we don't go to the pub for a beer but to Woolies to do our shopping; and Stirling has changed hands and is no longer licenced, so we don't pull in there either.

And I'm enjoying Friday Night Football again!"

Rod Turner is presently the manager at Landmark and has been for the past seven years since he came down from Mareeba.

"David Connolly managed the Roma branch before he became State Livestock Manager. It was David who offered me the transfer and I'm so pleased he did; I always wanted to manage Roma."

But Rod's association with Roma goes back to 1970 when he first came here as a cadet under Don Innes who Rod describes as a really inspirational leader.

"You'd be in the yards, absolutely buggered," recalls Rod, "and Don would come along and challenge you to a race up the lane. He was always cracking jokes and trying to make us see work as fun.

175

I try to do the same. You're out there on Monday night, sometimes all night, and if people can enjoy it, have a laugh while they're working, it makes for a happier team and keeps us all going.

It helps if you've got a natural fun-lover like Brad Vidler in the group, and of course I support him and encourage him. I think it's fair to say we look forward to our Monday nights.

And we've had some big ones. I'll always remember the 1st October 2002 when we had 6182 cattle out of 10,500 head. That yarding is on the front cover of this book.

At that time our team consisted of Rob Chapman, Matt Beard, Cheryl Bain and me, ably assisted by my son Tim who was then the branch manager at Mitchell.

We started drafting at 5.30am on Monday morning and there were no heads on pillows till we got the prices out after all the cattle were weighed at 3.00am Wednesday – 46 hours straight!

I like that. I like nothing more than auctioneering, selling cattle, the action environment of the saleyards; and I also like training young men who have the same passion.

At one stage we had three young blokes here, all Brads.

Brad Vidler came first then there was Brad Baker; for ready identification purposes we called them B1 and B2. Just after that Brad Passfield turned up so he became B3.

On one occasion we were selling a dairy cow, which is a pretty rare experience in Roma. She was as quiet as could be and I asked B2 to jump down off the catwalk and strip her out.

He scrambled down and grabbed the cow around the neck and it became very obvious he had no idea what I meant so B1 climbed down and milked her while B2 held on.

By the way, all three Bs turned out to be top young men.

I've been here a relatively short time but there have been many changes, many improvements; more selling pens for instance.

The computer setup has been upgraded, the yards have become EU accredited, bigger scales have been installed, they've overcome the problems with the scanners and the NLIS tags; there's something going on all the time.

Of course it's got to be like that if Roma is to stay No.1. The whole world is changing and we've got to change too or become obsolete like all those other saleyards that don't function any more.

Roma is unique; no other saleyards has the throughput, but we can expect further changes to keep up with the times and we can expect competition from rural entrepreneurs, but at the end of the day there will always be a Roma Saleyards.

I just want to be part of it.

I'm 55 now, my family is here, I have two sons here and I have grandchildren in the area. On top of that, I have a strong connection with Kidman and Consolidated and I love getting out, way out, to places like Innamincka and Birdsville to service those clients.

I like that style of work, I like training people, I like running the business, and I like Roma, so I guess I'll be here for a while yet."

Duncan McLeod has been an agent since 5th January 1981 when he started with Elders in the mailroom in Sydney. His 12½ years in NSW included 6½ years in Stud Stock before he moved up to Rockhampton so when he came to Roma in March 2000 it could be said he was a versatile agent with interstate experience.

"I came down here to take a position with Murray Arthur Agencies," says Duncan, "and I was very fortunate that Murray was willing to say up front that if things worked out a partnership arrangement would be available. And that is exactly what happened.

Murray was very true and straight to his word the whole way along. I progressed to becoming his partner and when he decided to call it a day in 2005, he sold out to me.

I have a silent partner, Karl Harms from Myall Charolais Stud; we've kept the name but we now trade simply as MAA, and Roma Saleyards, the greatest exchange centre for livestock in Australia, is an integral part of our operation.

The saleyards come in for a bit of criticism at times, we all know that there could be improvements, but it's streets ahead of whatever runs second.

Yesterday, I was talking to Tony White who was up here buying cattle. Now Tony is Elders State Livestock Manager in NSW and he has been to more saleyards than most people.

Tony says, that for the number of cattle that go through, for the way the job is handled, for the efficiency overall, it's not perfect but it's better than anything he's seen, it's a credit to everyone who works here, and we should appreciate the facility that we've got.

Coming from an outsider, I think that's worth recording!"

Brian Fisher is presently the local manager for Grant Daniel & Long. He says he has been an agent as long as he can remember which is fair enough because he started when he was 15 and he's now 43.

He did his first public auction at the age of eight when he sold the cakes at the school fete but when he was twelve and Billy Drummond gave him a run at a clearing sale, he really got the bug.

Brian has had a couple of stints in Roma and has put together a total of 15 years in and around the saleyards. He credits his present auction ability to the guidance of people like Brendan Wade, Garth Hughes and Blake Munro.

But his staccato style is unique; he's quicker than a machine gun. Tourists have remarked that he doesn't even breathe.

"Oh, I breathe alright," says Brian. "In through the nose and out through my mouth; they tell me it's the same technique they use to play the didgeridoo but I don't know about that, I never tried it.

Anyway, I like selling and so does my offsider Geoff Maslen. He won the Young Auctioneers trophy in Brisbane in 2006 and was just pipped for the national title in Sydney this year.

You're lucky in life if you can find a job that you really enjoy; that's how it is with me and auctioneering - and there is no better place for an auctioneer to be than Roma Saleyards."

Cyril Close came to Roma from Charters Towers in 1995.

His role in those days was as an auctioneer with Elders but since then he has been their Livestock Manager, the manager for Grant Daniel & Long and now, in partnership with his wife Sue, he has his own business, Close Marketing, as the franchisee for TopX.
I asked him about his experiences at the saleyards:

"Well I learned to do a lot of miles, on foot; learned to present cattle properly; learned to appreciate cattle from different areas, to work out which ones do and which ones don't, and learned to buy the right cattle for any given job.

Roma is the shop window of the cattle market in Australia these days and because we are here every week, I learned to appreciate values and to understand market trends.

For an agent to provide a full service you have to be, not only a manager, but also an auctioneer, a marketer and a buyer, and there is no better place to practice all that than at Roma.

I see every day at the saleyards as a challenge, that's what keeps you going, keeps you on your toes; it could be to get a premium rate for a particular line, or it could be getting cattle drafted to suit a certain specification.

Starting off the business from scratch I had to make sure to get the right staff and I'm very fortunate to have Carl Warren and Andrew Jensen, two well known honest and reliable men, one a bit younger that the other, but between us I think we make an all round team

And as far as enjoying it, well there are always plenty of laughs out here and if you can't get one you make one.

Lots of people wouldn't understand why we would want to be out here every day in all weathers, and some nights too, but this is my life as well as my business; this is what I do."

Brad Neven was born and bred at Injune where the family own cattle properties. He went to boarding school in Rockhampton and his first job was with Dalgetys in Charleville.

After two years he was transferred back to Roma under Val Harms and Mick Browne but he didn't stay with the firm and finished up as a trainee auctioneer at Watkins & Co. with Kevin Watkins and Peter Holland.

As time went by, Kevin retired and sold the business, Brad moved up through the ranks and he is now the Managing Director.

"In 20 years, you see a lot of changes in the industry, people come and go, and you meet a lot of characters. One such man was a bloke named Hector MacLaughlin who had a place up on the Taroom Road. I didn't know him well but they say he was a World War 1 veteran.

I'd only been there a couple of months, I was pretty new to the business, but Peter Holland had been talking to Hector and found out that he had cattle to sell so he got me to organise to bring them in.

Mouse explained to me that the facilities on the property were inadequate, that Hector himself may or may not be there, but that we were to organise to muster and tailtag the cattle, fill out the permit and arrange to have them trucked into the sale.

Well I got hold of Roy McIntosh and another local fella. They took out a couple of horses, arrived half an hour ahead of me and unloaded, and when I arrived I went up to the house to see Hector.

But I couldn't find him. I walked around the house, sung out a few times and when there was no answer I peeped in through the door.

There were three big bags of buffel stored in the lounge room, the bags had busted, seed had filled the lounge room to the depth of about one and a half or two foot, and foot traffic through the room had created what looked like cattlepads from one room to the next.

I just couldn't believe that this old fella could live like that!

Curiosity got the better of me. I walked in calling his name all the time and in another room I found these ports on the floor; they were open and you could see his old army uniforms. It was just as though he had never unpacked since he came back from the war.

The cattle were all in the house paddock and the boys soon had them under control; I hadn't found Hector so I jumped in the car and drove down to follow them up to the yards.

The next thing this old grey-haired bloke comes charging out of the timber on a tractor, waving a rifle and screaming:

"I'll shoot these bastards; they're pinchin' my cattle."

Anyway I managed to calm him down. That took 10 or 15 minutes but I was able to convince him that we were on his side and were only there to help him.

That certainly was an experience for a young agent!

Hector had an old ute that he used to drive into town. Every panel on the ute was dented; he'd hit guide posts, every guide post from the property to town they reckoned.

They said that if he wanted to buy fuel, he would pull up, fill up, hand over his cheque book for the attendant to fill in, then present his bank statement to show how much was there to cover the cheque.

He carried a few problems from the war, old Hector. He's long since gone now but he was one of the characters I'll never forget.

Later on, apart from selling cattle as an agent, I used to buy as well and I did a lot of buying for Bindaree and Yolarno.

At one stage I was buying cattle to go into the feedlot for Bindaree Beef and Terry Pyne of C. L. Squires & Co at Inverell was organising the feedlot side of the operation.

This day the sale started at 9 o'clock, the market was a bit tough and when Terry rang me around eleven and asked how I was going, I told him I had about 500 or a few more.

Well he just laughed and hung up.

At the end of the day he rang again:

"How many cattle did you finish up with; how many trucks will we need?"

"A fair few," I replied.

"What's the total?"

"1876!"

He nearly fell off the phone.

"1876? Why didn't you ring me, why didn't you warn me?

"Well I told you at eleven o'clock we had 500, you told me to keep going and laughed, and here we are with 1876!"

"Shit; I'd better get off the phone, book some trucks and find some feedlot space."

They tell me it's the most cattle bought by one buyer with one order at Roma Saleyards. But I wouldn't know about that; haven't been here long enough.

But enough of that! There is nothing more pleasing than to stand up on the rail and sell cattle for a vendor at a premium price and see them walk away from the yards smiling.

We may have seen a lot of sad faces in the last six months with the drought and all; it does get a bit hard at times and it hurts me to see people hurting, but rain will change all that and in the meantime, where else would you sell 'em but here.

As far as I'm concerned it's the only cattle selling centre in Australia. All roads lead to Roma!

Andrew Jensen first came to the saleyards as a youth 30 years ago to help his father, Ron Jensen, who worked as a stockman at that time.

Later on he bought for ACC and for 13 years he was a major buyer at every sale to the extent of around 30,000 cattle annually.

Now he has become an agent working for TopX and I asked him how he was handling the transition from buyer to agent:

There not a great deal of difference. The cattle are the same, the people are the same, but you have to be a little more considerate of other agents; you probably can't be such a smart-arse!

181

You have to be a little more tactful with your vendors, you can't be blunt with them talking about the cattle they have bred, you must realise that their livelihood is involved, and you have to respect their feelings.

The commission is important but it's far more important to realise you are doing a job for the client who has entrusted you with his livelihood.

Buying is sport, it's competitive, it's like playing football or something, and I really enjoyed that sort of sporting competition, but I'm also enjoying what I do now.

I enjoy the cattle industry and working with all the types of people in it, and I'm enjoying my role as an agent more and more.

I buggerise around a bit at times and I can be a bit facetious, but when you're either buying or selling cattle you have to remember that you are responsible for someone else's money, someone's livelihood, and you have to take your job seriously.

And that's how I feel about it!

Don Turner came out of semi-retirement to rejoin Dalgetys in Roma as Livestock Manager after a lengthy career with the same company including 10 years as their senior auctioneer at Newmarket saleyards in Melbourne.

With him came a wealth of experience and a unique auction style, in fact many rated him the best fat cattle auctioneer in Roma.

I asked him why he gave it up:

I considered auctioneering as just part of the job. There is a lot more involved than standing up on the catwalk and selling. It's the end bit, the climax, but a helluva lot goes on before you can start selling.

Anyway, age catches up with us all and unfortunately it has certainly caught up with me. That happens!

I was feeding cattle as a contractor for seven years but I'm giving that away too; you can't get hay!

But I still do a bit for the old firm behind the scenes; I still do some of the bookwork and check their cattle as they go across the scales to make sure the delivery is right. I still keep in touch.

It's a good setup here. Those who are critical of these yards need to be reminded of the numbers. No set of yards in Australia was built to handle 12,000 head yet we've had that many through here.

Saleyards everywhere attract characters and no doubt you have mentioned a few in your book, but looking back over the years I remember one old bloke at Newmarket who was about 82; his name was Frank and he worked for Jimmy Matthews.

As you know, the entire area at Newmarket was paved with bluestone cobblestones about a foot square and nearly as deep.

Someone came up to Frank and says:

"How long have you been here?"

"See them cobblestones?"

"Yeah!"

"Well that's the third set since I've been here."

Before we leave Don and his memories it's worth recording that he had a lot to do with the Meat Exporters Golf Day held in Roma every November.

The annual game between buyers and agents was on the social calendar before Don arrived but it was Don and Darryl Harland that really got it going.

In recent years there have been up to 160 players competing for $3000 worth of trophies and prizes so you can see they were able to turn it into a really big event.

But Rod Turner (no relation to Don), the present manager of Landmark in Roma, has the final word on this long-serving agent:

"Don Turner was one of the most capable men who ever worked for Dalgetys. He would have more ability in one little finger than most blokes have in their whole bodies."

Steve "The Sparrow" Goodhew has been an agent in Roma for 13 years. He started with Primac but is now with P.J. Holland & Co.

Firstly, we discussed the name "Sparrow" and how he acquired a name like that and as far as Steve could remember it was the brainchild of Jimmy Green.

So I checked with Jimmy and, yes, he agreed he invented the title on the basis that 'the sparrow is seldom seen in the bush and is a nuisance in town'.

How that could apply to Steve I wouldn't know but the name has certainly stuck and there would be people who know him only as "The Sparrow" the No.1 man working for "The Mouse".

You could only have a combination like that at the saleyards!

This is Steve's story:

Ever since I was a schoolboy I wanted to be in the agency game and I started out with Primac straight from school, worked in a few branches with them and ended up in Roma, but I've been with Peter now for 10 years.

I thoroughly enjoy what I do. Every day is different, there's always a new challenge in the job and one phone call can decide what you might be doing from one day to the next.

You are meeting new people all the time, contacts become your clients, clients become your friends, and you find that you are doing business seven days a week.

My hobbies include camp-drafting and a led steer that's won a few prizes. I'm taking him to the Brisbane Exhibition this year.

With those activities you find you are meeting a lot of different people, all potential clients, so you are mixing business with pleasure and that's good.

But to come out here to the saleyards is probably the highlight of the week. For a small private agency we have a solid share of the market but apart from selling cattle you can be guaranteed of a laugh or at least a bit of excitement every sale.

I remember the time when I was up on the catwalk selling and Johnny McMahon's teasing finally drove John McNally over the edge.

McNally took his glasses off, put them away and prepared to knock McMahon's head off but they were both past doing any real damage, blows were never landed and calm was restored.

The scuffle did have the very positive effect of shutting McMahon up for the rest of the day and that suited us all.

Anyway, I'd like to think I'd be around here for a long time yet; this'll do me!

Justin Stivano has been an agent in Roma for 11 years.

He came here as an auctioneer with Murray Arthur, started his own private agency, J.H. Stivano Livestock Marketing, worked in with Watkins & Co as an auctioneer, and now these days he works as an auctioneer on Tuesdays under contract to Elders.

You might gather from the above that his auctioneering services are in demand, but he says it's not easy and if there was an easier way to make money he'd be doing it.

Auctioneers are in the best position to see exactly what goes on at a cattle sale and I suggested to Justin that he would have seen some funny things at times and had some interesting experiences:

There would be million and one things, sometimes you get your knickers in a knot, sometimes it's not all beer and skittles, but the most vivid recollection I have of an incident in these yards goes back before they started weighing the stores.

You'll remember in those days cattle were still sold dollars per head and how the buyers had to let their own cattle out of the selling pens, marshal them up and get them down the lanes into a water yard.

There would be a dozen blokes all trying to do the same thing in the same lane at the same time, it wasn't hard to box cattle or cut someone off and nerves got a bit frayed on a regular basis.

This day a father and son combination had bought cattle and the young bloke decided to start letting the cattle out on his own.

Well he got some of his out but also made the mistake of letting some of Val Harms' purchases out too and he had them all boxed up in the lane when Val arrived.

You can't print what was said, I'll leave that to the reader's imagination, but let me tell you that Val gave the young man the greatest dressing down I've witnessed and when his father turned up he gave him a serve too even suggesting the son should not have been born … in words that meant the same.

Well all this produced the right effect in that the father and son buying team was a bit more careful letting cattle out in future.

It would be unreasonable to expect this chapter to contain the stories of all agents that had ever worked in Roma; on the other hand I think it's only fair that all today's agents should at least be mentioned as being here when the book was printed.

The **Watkins & Co** livestock team consists of Brad Neven, local identity Jimmy Green and Rex Wells from Wallumbilla. Brad does most of the selling but Rex has his auctioneer's licence now and lends a hand at times. Bryan Hickey comes out on sale days to do the books.

Ray White Rural is about to have a change of ownership with founder Daven Vohland selling his share to Jack Clanchy who will become Rob Wildermuth's new partner.

185

In the **TopX** camp, apart from Cyril Close who owns the business, there is Andrew Jensen who was previously buying for ACC, and budding young auctioneer Carl Warren who was placed in the 2006 Young Auctioneers competition and who took out the prestigious Mike Nixon award in Queensland.

Duncan McLeod is the boss at **MAA** and he is supported by David Murray in Roma and Seamus Filan in Mitchell as well as a couple of boundary riders further out.

Rod Turner is the manager at **Landmark** and he does most of the selling himself. His right hand man is Brad Vidler who has twice been placed in the Queensland Young Auctioneers Competition. Then there is Andrew Holt, Injune manager Tony Bowen who is here every sale day and who also takes his turn at selling, and Don Turner.

Peter "The Mouse" Holland owns and manages **P.J. Holland & Co** and his No.1 man and auctioneer is Steve "Sparrow" Goodhew. They are ably supported at the yards and in the field by veteran stockman Barry Hughes and trainee auctioneer Jeremy Cahill.

At **Grant, Daniel & Long**, Brian Fisher is the manager and senior auctioneer, Geoff Maslen, the Queensland Young Auctioneer 2006 champion is his worthy assistant, Travis Holland has recently joined the team, and Jason Belz is based in Augathella.

The **Elders** team: Peter McDonald, manager, Tim McNamara, livestock manager and auctioneer, Terry Hyland, Dane Pearce, Mick Connell, George & Shirley Ayers, Justin Stivano, Rodney Doig (Mitchell) and Don Kelly (Injune).

9. Points of Interest

No matter where you go in the world or what you see, you'll miss certain points of interest unless they are pointed out and explained by one of the locals. So too at Roma Saleyards:

The Duke's Gate: The year 2001 was to have been a big year at Roma Saleyards. Royalty, in the presence of Prince Phillip the Duke of Edinburgh, was to make an appearance.

Queen Elizabeth II was coming to open the award winning Big Rig Tourist and Information Centre and, while Her Royal Highness attended to those duties, Prince Phillip was to visit the saleyards.

The chosen date was a Tuesday, the weekly store sale would be in progress, the Duke would be up there on the catwalk with the auctioneer, there would be world-wide media coverage, the publicity would be enormous, and everyone was excited months in advance of the big event.

The market reporter got on the ABC and told "Macca on a Sunday Morning"; Macca got excited too and all over Australia the news went out that the Duke was coming to Roma Saleyards.

But first we had to have a visit from the heavies of Buckingham Palace to check the security, to make sure all was in order, that everything was safe, that the Duke would be unharmed; after all, he was over eighty and unused to saleyard catwalks.

As a result of their inspections, changes were made.

Firstly, where the Duke would descend the steps to the catwalk, the wooden treads were quite narrow and the steps themselves quite steep, there was the danger that the old gentleman might slip and break his neck, so a nice new set of gently sloping steel steps was installed.

Secondly, the existing pedestrian entrances were just not up to royal standards. One gate from the car park was adjacent to the storm water drain and the selling pens and was considered to be out of the way, whereas the other led directly to the corridor past the toilets, and that just wouldn't do.

A brand new gate was needed, the Duke's Gate, so a hole was cut in the wire fence, a concrete step was laid, and all was in readiness to welcome His Royal Highness the Duke of Edinburgh in October.

But then came September 11th 2001 and the terrorist attacks on New York, the world was in upheaval and all royal travel plans were cancelled.

The Duke never came, he never used that gate; everybody else did and subsequent traffic destroyed the lawn, but he did come to Roma in March 2002 and he opened the Big Rig Tourist Centre but it was not on a saleday so we missed him at the yards.

In 2007, the old fence was taken down and replaced by a more fashionable lower model, but they kept the opening the Duke would have used had he come to Roma Saleyards, so that we can all remember what might have been … and you and I don't have to walk past the dunnies either!

The Bench near the Scale House Door: Up on the steel platform that overlooks the pens leading to the scales there is a bench, just an ordinary wooden bench for people to sit on. But it has a story:

Pioneer transport operator Fergus Williams, who was getting on a bit and approaching 100 years, was up there talking with Barrie Loughnan, ex Shire Chairman, ex Saleyards Board President and now the unofficial "Ambassador of Roma Saleyards".

History does not recall the topics of conversation but you can nearly bet there was mention of how things used to be done and the changes that had been made since Ferg started carting cattle here in his semi-trailer in 1939.

At that time there was no bench, so when Ferg said that it would be nice to be able to sit down, as people approaching 100 like to sit down now and then, there was no place for him to sit.

Well the next day, the old Shire Chairman spoke to the new Shire Chairman - who happened to be his son, Rob Loughnan, who was also President of the Saleyards Board - and the next thing you know there was a bench for Ferg and everybody else to sit on.

Because of its proximity to the scales and all the weighing action, it attracts visitors from all over the world and has become a great spot to take group photos.

Barrie Loughnan told me all of this himself, so it must be right, and his story brought back memories of Ireland, specifically the stone outside the door of Dan Murphy's pub in Sneem, County Kerry.

The door opens out onto a sort of beer garden where people gather on sunny days and drink Guinness, sing songs and enjoy life.

Right beside the door is a stone, big enough for three or four people to sit on at once and on the wall behind it is this poem:

The Stone Outside Dan Murphy's Door

Those days in our hearts
We will cherish
Contented altho we were poor
And the songs that were sung
In the days we were young
On the stone outside
Dan Murphy's Door

SNEEM, COUNTY KERRY, IRELAND.

And I thought to meself, "Our bench at Roma Saleyards deserves a poem like that."

Well Lurelle had a go and came up with:

The Saleyards Bench

These days at the yards we will treasure
We're hard working but happy too
There are deeds that are done
And tales that are spun
On the bench near the scale-house door.

At Roma Saleyards
The Biggest Cattle Selling Centre in Australia

Then I had a go and wrote these lines:

The Bench Overlooking the Scales

People from around the world
Are welcome at our auction
To see the cattle go over the scales
And take in all the action.
But rest a while on this bench
Sit and talk a bit
And spare a thought for Fergus Williams
The man who suggested it!

Now, we would be the first to agree that there would be better verses out there, something that would really capture the atmosphere and the vibe of the place.

You have a go, send us your poem and once we have the best of the bunch we'll pass it on to "The Ambassador", to talk to the Chairman, to talk to the Board ... and next time you come to Roma Saleyards it'll be there ... behind the bench near the scale-house door!

The Trees of Knowledge: In main streets of most country towns there is a tree where people gather in the shade to sit and talk and watch the world go by.

Wise old men gather under such tree on a regular basis and it is quite common to refer to the tree as "The Tree of Knowledge"; in fact in some bush towns there is a sign to that effect.

There is no such tree in Roma; the place to be is on a bench in the air-conditioning at Woolies where you'll see all the old blokes exchanging lies. But there is such a tree at the saleyards.

In fact there are five Athel Pine trees that shade benches and rocks where wise people sit and talk about the market and the weather, and the weather and the market, and wile away the time in pleasant company. And so it is said that there are five "Trees of Knowledge" at Roma Saleyards.

Buy why five, you ask?

That's because more wise people come to Roma Saleyards and they need the extra shade to accommodate them all!

The Memorial Plaques: Certain blokes who aren't with us any more are remembered by three plaques mounted on the wall of the office building. These were erected when Keith Kimlin was Superintendent and full credit to him for the idea:

The first plaque was erected in 1989 to remember five men who died in a plane crash. They were returning to Roma at night from a sale at Longreach, the weather was bad and the charter plane went down just north of town killing all on board.

They were Noel Allom from Dalgetys Roma, Max McCauley from Elders Eidsvold, Bruce Temple from Elders Wallumbilla, Wilson Millar "Tecoma" Wallumbilla, and the pilot Fernando Rossi.

May they rest in peace!

190

The second one is in memory of Ross Stewart, known as "The Colt", who was the manager of Primac, Roma. On the 27th November 1990, a sale day, Ross was there all day, did his business, went home and took the dog to obedience school.

And dropped dead, just like that!

Mick Connell, and others who were around in those days, remember him as top agent, a fair dinkum bloke, and one whose death came as a real shock.

The third plaque is for Doug Wilson whose lengthy involvement with the saleyards is mentioned in Chapter 5.

Doug is typical of all those long-serving stockmen who served the saleyards so well for so long; the unsung heroes of the industry who operate behind the scenes away from the limelight.

Without blokes like Doug Wilson, Roma Saleyards would never have become what it is today.

And if they ever name the road from the highway to the saleyards, I'd like to see it named "Doug Wilson Drive"!

10. Tourists & Visitors

Visitors to Roma Saleyards come from all over the world ... and other parts as well, as my old mate John "Barty" Barrett would say.

Get up on that high platform any sale day between April and October when big numbers of tourists are on the move, speak to the strangers, ask them where they are from, and you'll realise that's true.

On that viewing platform one day I took a group photo of the Grade 2 and 3 pupils from Miles State School seated on the bench near the scale-house door.

On the way back to the canteen I met a couple from Calgary in Canada, a man from Zimbabwe, a bloke from Adelaide, two young people from Switzerland and two from Scotland ... and there were just as many that I didn't meet.

In the last few years I have had the pleasure of meeting hundreds of such people and now you can meet some of them too:

Joe & Julie Perry, Over Peover, Cheshire, England, first landed in Perth on New Years Day in 2003 and spent three months in Australia visiting southern states in a campervan and finished up in Brisbane.

The weather was lousy so they travelled inland to Inglewood, Texas and Lightning Ridge then headed back towards Brisbane to catch their flight home.

Julie Perry wrote this story in 2007:

We read in our travel guide that the biggest Australian cattle sales were held in Roma. Joe had always been a cattleman having worked on farms in England and we had hoped to see something of Australian cattle stations on our trip, so we set off to Roma, arrived on a Wednesday evening and discovered there was a sale the next day.

We really enjoyed the auctioneers and observing the cattle being moved about. Joe took photos from the public viewing platform and we even went down in the lanes among the buyers to have a closer look at the cattle. It was exciting.

Talking to locals we learned there was a bigger sale coming up the following Tuesday. We were running out of time but we decided to stay in this friendly place till then. We are so glad we did.

The store sale really opened our eyes – the thousands of cattle, the distances they travelled, the speed of the auction – and the steak sandwiches in the canteen were the best we had ever tasted.

The market reporter took our photo, we were featured in the "Western Star" newspaper as "Visitors from England", we felt very important, and when we left that day we decided that on our next trip to Australia we would start in Roma and head further west from there and so see the real Australia where all those cattle came from.

And that's what happened. Two years later we landed in Brisbane and came straight to Roma. The numbers in the store sale had swelled to over 10,000, the hospitality was the same, the steak sandwiches were as good as ever, and the market reporter remembered us from last time. It was good to be back.

From there we headed to Longreach, Cloncurry, stayed on a huge cattle station at Burketown - Joe even helped with the cattle in the yards and drove their truck - then we went across to Darwin and Broome and on down to Perth and back home.

We will always be so glad that by sheer coincidence we went to Roma Saleyards … and we intend to come back!

Steen & Ingrid Dethlefsen live in Adelaide, South Australia. They had a good day out and sent this note:

"It was such an experience to visit the saleyards on our way to the Gold Coast. We really enjoyed the visit and have told our friends and workmates; they were all very impressed!"

Noel & Rosemary Oliver are from Launceston in Tasmania. Noel was a wool buyer and knows all about auctions and they have both been to cattle sales before, but what they saw at Roma was a different experience as Noel explains:

"It is a really amazing setup – the horsemen, the weighing, the gates that work by remote control, the efficiency of the system, and to be able to get up on the viewing platform and see all the action, it's a real eye-opener; we've never seen horsemen working in saleyards before, then again we've never been in yards as big as these.

We'll be telling others; this is a 'must see' for anyone wanting to get a feel for the real Australia."

Lincoln & Carla Romero are from Brazil. Carla first came to Roma as a Rotary Exchange student in 1985 and stayed with Barry & Sue McCabe. In 2005 she returned with husband Lincoln and daughters Giulia & Laura and they all visited the saleyards.

Janet & Angus Davidson came out from Pontypool in Wales and visited the saleyards in company with their friends Reg & Beryl Gibbs from Murwillumbah NSW. Their story goes like this:

We come out to Australia now and again and do a trip in a caravan that we leave at Murwillumbah with Reg & Beryl.

We were coming up the Toowoomba Range when the car broke down. We managed to get onto the RACQ but while they were coming, a young bloke on his way to a wedding, pulled up, stuck his head under the bonnet and got the car started but it died again before we could put it into gear.

We were in a bad spot, on a bit of a bend and the tail of the van was blocking half a lane so it was quite dangerous really.

Anyway, along comes this truck, a big cattle truck, and pulls up right behind us. The driver hops out, big smile all over his face, and he says,

"Would you like a tow?"

Hadn't really thought about being towed by a cattle truck, which I know now was a Frasers B-Double, but it seemed a good idea to get out of the spot we were in as soon as we could.

So we agreed and he pulled around in front of us then backed back close enough to tie a rope onto the car. You can imagine what all this was doing to the traffic flow and the next thing the police arrived.

But when the constable realised what the Frasers man was doing, he fully agreed and helped divert other vehicles till the truck-trailer-car-and-caravan unit were ready to roll.

The truck was empty so he had no weight to carry which allowed him plenty of power to take us up to the top of the range and he dropped us off at the Mobil where we were able to have the car repaired.

That took a while. Two hours later, the same Frasers truck came past again heading down the range fully loaded this time and the driver gave us a wave and a toot as he went past.

He was a real gentleman of the road; in fact the other chap on the way to a wedding was a real gentleman too. We still can't get over their friendship and hospitality. We felt very welcome in your country.

It was exciting to hear the story and they were pleased to tell it, but they said they were disappointed they didn't get the driver's name.

As it turned out Frasers Client Liaison Officer, Tim Clifford, was at the sale that day and once he had the date and time of day it only took him half an hour to identify the helpful driver as Scott Warden who lives at Westbrook when he's not driving trucks.

But that's not the end of the story!

The Davidsons contacted Scott to thank him; they kept in touch and a firm friendship developed. When Scott married Kristy, the Davidsons sent a wedding present from Wales and these days the couples exchange emails and phone calls on a regular basis.

And the world is a better place!

Mick & Kath Chester are from Wallsend in NSW. Mick was in the Police Service during his working life and had never been to a cattle sale till the day he came to Roma:

"I couldn't understand the auctioneer. He spoke in what sounded like Chinese, waved his arms about a lot, got really excited then stopped and gave himself a clap; it was all very strange.

Then we met this market reporter bloke and he explained what was going on. He showed us how the buyers bid by chasing flies off their shoulder, flicking a silver pen or winking at the auctioneer, and he got me that way that I wasn't game to adjust my hat for fear of finishing up with a truck load.

It became very interesting. We learned that the clap meant the cattle had been sold and we discovered that one buyer was taking cattle down our way to Scone to be slaughtered.

It was a great morning and we took lots of photos but photos can't convey the atmosphere; nothing is as good as the real thing."

As she left, Kath made the remark:

"Mick wanted to go to the saleyards and see the cattle sale but I thought how boring it would be, and smelly too.

But I'm so glad I came; it's been the highlight of our holiday."

Robert Knott is from Zimbabwe. I met him at the saleyards in 2004.

Knotts have been in South Africa since 1820; they originally came from Kent in England. In the 1960s, Robert's father shifted his family up to Rhodesia (now Zimbabwe) and Robert grew up at "Midlands Ranch" Belingwe (now Mberengawa). In 1976 Robert went into a cattle partnership with his younger brother Andrew and by 2004, the brothers ran 6,000 head.

Robert is married to Noeline and they have two youngsters, Johanna and Thomas. This is his story:

"We have been here a long time and I could handle Zimbabwe," he says, "but there's no future for children so we had to get out."

"In April 2004 I came to Australia, landed in Sydney, toured Queensland, stopped over in Roma because I was told it was good cattle country, spent an interesting few hours at Roma Saleyards and was impressed, subscribed to the Queensland Country Life, flew to Adelaide, then Perth, then back home.

Later in 2005, Noeline and I were back in Brisbane heading for Roma but as we had read an interesting article *Buying Your First Farm – Is It Viable?* by Dr Geoff Slaughter of Queensland University Gatton Campus in the Country Life, we called there first.

We met the editor Mark Phelps, he introduced us to Stan Wallace, Stan and his wife Margaret joined us for a working breakfast, he took us to dinner to meet more people, then he gave us introductions to Graham 'Gravelly' Henderson in Dalby and 'The Mouse' in Roma. We couldn't get over the reception; it was unbelievable!

You can't take money out of Zimbabwe so we could only afford a modest start. We looked at properties at Dalby, Dulacca and Roma, toured Central Queensland but ended up back at Roma.

You drive into a town as a stranger and you know instinctively if you'll like the place; by this time we had virtually decided we would come to Roma to start our new life.

By the end of 2005 we had signed a lease on Janice Colley's 'Wyndella', nice house on good country just 10km on the bitumen out of Roma; this would be our base, Johanna and Thomas could go to school, we could run a few cattle and by May '06 we had settled in.

We are very glad to be here. We have bought a few cattle at the saleyards, we have also sold a few there, everyone has been helpful and friendly and we are starting to feel part of the place.

And the good news is that the lengthy immigration process is reaching finality as this book goes to print."

Good on you, Robert; good on you, Noeline.
Welcome to Australia; welcome to Roma!

STOP PRESS: Robert's brother, Andrew, was married recently. If that union is blessed with children, will we see more Knotts out here?

Ron & Margaret Lloyd from Albany, in W.A. wrote after their visit:
"We arrived home last week after three months and 13,500kms on the road. Thank you for the Roma paper – that's the first time we've ever made a cattle sales page."

Paulo & Ana Lima are from Portugal. They dropped in on the way past just for a quick look:
"It's like a well-oiled machine. We were pleased to see how the cattle are handled, with decency and respect, and the whole place is so clean and the people are very friendly.

We only had a short time but we could feel the pulse of the place … this is the real thing."

Bill Storman from Toogoolawah called into the store sale on his way home from visiting his son who is a helicopter pilot in Cloncurry.
"I'd heard about Roma Saleyards and I just had to have a look. I've seen plenty of cattle sales in my time, but nothing like this."

Alan Fraser from Scotland cut his teeth in Australia working for Ralph & Elizabeth Russell "Brides Creek" Blackall in 1990 during the time of the Charleville floods. He was floodbound for the first three weeks at Brides Creek and learned a bit about isolation and eating mutton, among other things.

The experience must have done him the world of good because back home he landed a very good job with the Scottish equivalent of the DPI and has since risen through the ranks to executive status.

In 2006, while travelling to New Zealand with a mate named Paul Grant and before returning to Scotland, the lads decided on a week-long stopover flying in to and out of Brisbane. This is Alan's story of the visit.

There were several reasons for the diversion: Paul wanted to visit an old schoolmate on Mt Tamborine, I wanted to visit John and Lurelle Gilfoyle who found me the job at Brides Creek, we both wanted to see Roma Saleyards … and also, we were looking for wives!

Our arrival coincided with the tail end of the Tuesday store sale and we left after the fat sale on the Thursday. Although both of us come from a farming and livestock haulage background and have very close links to the auction system in Scotland, we were amazed by the scale and efficiency of the operation.

Although distinctly different in appearance, the quality of the cattle was apparent and it was great to see such large even lines.

The welcome we received that night as complete strangers was absolutely first class and led to an invite from Allen Spinks and Melissa Jensen from Frasers Transport to go out in the truck and pick up cattle for the fat sale from Adrian Tiller's place "Siwa" south of town on the Wednesday.

It was a perfect day trip particularly for Paul, who in partnership with his father, runs two livestock and general haulage trucks and a great insight for both of us to experience the challenges of farming in such an environment.

After the fat sale we visited the Killara Feedlot - not much chance of finding a wife there - then Tamworth Country and Music Festival, Guyra Lamb and Potato Festival, Surfers Paradise for a night and rounded off the week with a night out in Noosa.

We met up with old friends, made some new ones and saw a lot of interesting countryside but our visit to Roma Saleyards was the highlight.

STOP PRESS: Paul has found himself a lady and although not married yet they are very happy together. Ironically, even in Scottish terms, she is practically his next door neighbour; he would have passed her farm in his truck every day for years.

Alan has been promoted to headquarters in Edinburgh; he is selling his house in Ayr, will have to buy again in Edinburgh, and he's still single ... and still looking!

Colin List from Monto was the leader of the Monto Landcare Group that visited the Maranoa district over three days; the saleyards was their last port of call:

"We've seen a lot of things, we've really enjoyed ourselves here, we've found the people very friendly, but the visit to the saleyards was definitely the highlight of the whole trip."

Janelle Allison and Doug Graham came from the Gatton Campus of the University of Queensland in 2006 with a group of their overseas students from China, the Philippines, Vietnam, Zambia and Tanzania

In 2007 they were back, this time with students from Papua New Guinea, the Philippines, New Zealand, Tanzania and Sri Lanka.

When asked why they come to Roma Saleyards they replied:

This is a particularly interesting place to bring our international agricultural students. Here they very quickly get an impression of the Australian cattle industry and they begin to appreciate how vast it is.

And we'll be back. We evaluate these excursions and the students rate the visit to your saleyards as the highlight of their trip.

Freek & Rina Ykema are from the Netherlands. They were at the store sale in April and Freek recorded these comments:

"It's beautiful. I especially enjoy the atmosphere of the whole market, the cows, seeing the real Australia, the blokes with the big cows, also thinking about the enormous change that young men and boys are going through in Australia.

This is Roma, this is the old Australia, but you don't see things like this in Brisbane or in Melbourne. I think it must be very hard for young men to grow up in a country that is changing so fast but here it's still traditional.

A hundred years ago, fifty years ago, there were pioneers in Australia but nowadays all of a sudden there are no real pioneers but people can still retain the feel of it out here with the cows.

It would be a tough life, I think, and that's why it's so nice to see so many men, doing the work they are doing and being happy.

199

They don't sit down and talk, they seem to me to take the attitude that the job has to be done and they go out and do it.

We are both from a country background, we still feel it in our blood, we can relate to all this and I think it's a pity that so many young people today, they miss out on this, they don't know that milk comes from cows."

"When you spoke of 'the atmosphere', what did you mean?"

"It's hard to put into words but you have the smell, the all pervading smell, the sound of the cows, the activity, the action, the noise of the auction; you can't describe it, you have to be here!"

"Would you recommend it as a tourist destination?"

"Most definitely! This is the real Australia."

Cal & Patti Callen have a saying: "We'll never get lost 'cause we don't know where we're going."

They come from the United States. He used to be a sheriff in Bucks County, Pennsylvania, and she is the Assistant Nurse Manager of a big Trauma Unit at North Broward Medical Center in Florida.

Interesting people!

They came to Australia with every intention of keeping away from cities and getting to meet the people in the bush. And so they came to Roma Saleyards … and stayed six days!

We are so pleased we did. This is what we wanted to see, these are the sort of people we wanted to meet and we met some characters and really enjoyed the experience, that's why we stayed so long.

On the Sunday before the sale we went out to the saleyards to have a look around and got to know Trevor Beck, the foreman, and Melissa Jensen who runs the Roma depot of Frasers Transport.

Trevor is really a bikie. He has a bald head and a beard so he seemed a bit out of place, but what a lovely man and such a hard worker. And Melissa, well she is the only woman running a big livestock trucking business.

They both made us feel very welcome and answered all our questions and we learned quite a lot about the operation from them.

We went out again on Monday night to see 9000 cattle get ready for saleday and ran into a big impressive agent named Rod Turner and he explained how the cattle are drafted and penned.

On Tuesday we were there all day. It was wonderful. All the noise, the auction, the buyers, the cattle going over the scales, the smell of the place – what an atmosphere!

We met people like 97-year-old Dexter Kruger and sat with him under the Trees of Knowledge while he recited poetry about how he dipped the deer in the Conondale Ranges a long time ago.

There was an agent, Glen Nielsen. What a man! We could have spent the whole day with him. He introduced us to his brother Garry who has a property at Morven. The people here are so friendly!

It was interesting to see the various breeds of cattle and how well they were handled. And you have to admire the efficiency of the entire operation – we were impressed.

I don't know where else you would find people with the guts to keep going like we see here. No matter what the hardships, they enjoy each other, they enjoy family, and there is respect for the land and respect for each other.

We came here to Roma not only to see but to absorb, to smell the cattle, to breathe the atmosphere, to be in touch with reality; it all goes to make our hearts feel pretty good.

But it's all about the people. The weather is beautiful, the land is lovely but it's dry, it's hard and you need rain. But it's not taking anybody down. Everybody here is in good spirits, enjoying each others company and business goes on as usual.

And we are very much impressed in passing through that people have the time to talk to us, to stop and say "Hi", and we hope that some of the people will come visit us.

But we'll return to this great land, we'll be back in Australia as soon as funds allow … and we'll come back to Roma Saleyards!

Graham & Jill McFadzen were at the saleyards one morning with forty or more members of the Nashos Touring Club. This happy group of ex National Servicemen and their partners spend time together on the road once a year and on this occasion they had 10 days in Roma.

Graham has carted cattle to the saleyards at Eumundi, Maleny and Kenilworth in his time and they both had some experience with cattle before they came so it was not totally foreign to them.

After a couple of hours at the fat sale, they commented:

It's bigger than Maleny! Absolutely magnificent! A real credit to the town! We have never seen anything like this before - the whole arrangement, they way it all works, how you can stand over the scales and watch them go through, it is absolutely fantastic.

Everybody should come and have a look to get to understand the cattle industry. We'll be telling all our friends for sure.

Jim & Glyn Wilson are from Melbourne. They were on their annual three-month tour when they called in:

We've been to Queensland plenty of times before but never to your saleyards, or any other saleyards for that matter. We read about it in a tourist brochure and timed our journey to be in Roma on a sale day.

It's just been a fabulous experience; we've enjoyed it so much. Meeting "Barrie the Ambassador" helped enormously because he explained things to us so we knew what was happening.

And just seeing a different way of life, very different to anything we have been used to; seeing the cattle, seeing the organisation, the horsemen taking the cattle up through the lanes, seeing the weighing, the things we never even thought about.

Getting down among the buyers in the lane gave us a feeling of being part of it all and we meet some wonderful people, interesting people - buyers, sellers, agents – and the auctioneers, they're fascinating, they just don't stop, they don't even breathe.

How do they do that?

It's all so orderly. We didn't expect it to be so well organised, but it has to be when you think about it with all those cattle. We really came not knowing what to expect and we're so pleased we did. We have thoroughly enjoyed the whole experience.

We've had a wonderful morning topped off with a delicious steak sandwich in the canteen as recommended by Barrie.

Today is going down as the highlight of our trip.

John & Marlene Freeman live at Golden Beach, Caloundra, since John retired from the Air Force at Amberley. They were heading west and called into the saleyards one Thursday during the sale.

"It's terrific," said Marlene. "I don't know anything about cattle, but the organisation here is so thorough, the way they move all the cattle around is incredible, and the agents and stockmen are so proficient."

202

"I'm quite stunned," was John's comment. "I realised this was a very large operation but I was stunned to see it all actually unfold.

The number of cattle that are here, the way they are handled, from selling to weighing, trucking in trucking out, it's an unbelievably complex system that works so perfectly.

I may never get the chance to come this way again, but if I did come back I would have my friends here. We are in a caravan club and it would be great to be able to show all this to other people."

Janelle & Pearce Phelps and their cousin **Tiarna Phelps** come from "Woodburn" Roma and "Warrie" St George respectively. They visited the saleyards during Christmas school holidays in 2005 with their fathers, regular buyers, Tim and John Phelps.

In my job as market reporter, I'm always looking for new subjects to photograph and I send the photos with the reports to various rural newspapers.

There is usually a spare photo or two and these are sent to the people who were good enough to allow me to take the shot.

The three cousins were perched up on the top rail in the lane as I went past, the photo was taken, it finished up in the paper, and a couple of spare prints were subsequently posted to the Phelps families.

This sort of thing happens every week, twice a week in fact, and over the years I have received many thank you letters, phone calls, emails and cards from a host of grateful people especially from wives whose husbands never have the time to have their photo taken.

Grandmothers like them too. I have lost count of the number of grandparents who ring up asking for a copy of a photo and they are really pleased to get their hands on a picture of their grandkids.

Mind you, we get as much fun out of all this as the people themselves; that's really why we keep doing it!

And with the writing, we get an enormous amount of pleasure out of the joy it brings to others. That someone else is having a laugh is far more rewarding to us than the financial side.

Happiness comes by way of feedback in the mail, by phone, by email or a kind word at the saleyards.

Anyway, we get lots of thank-you notes … but the best one we have ever received was sent by Janelle and Pearce Phelps after their photo arrived at "Woodburn" … and if you read the letter on the next page you'll see what I mean!

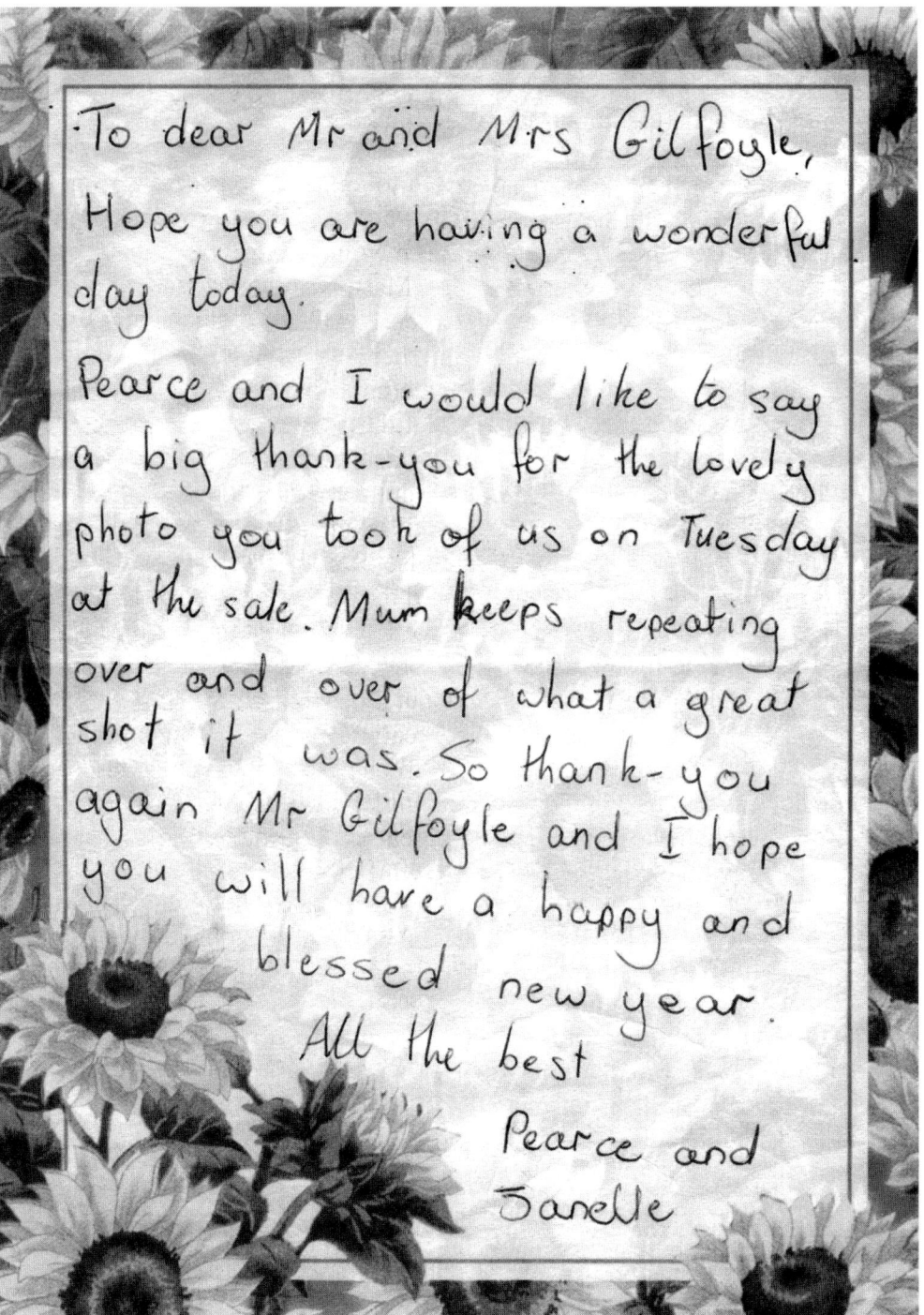

To dear Mr and Mrs Gilfoyle,

Hope you are having a wonderful day today.

Pearce and I would like to say a big thank-you for the lovely photo you took of us on Tuesday at the sale. Mum keeps repeating over and over of what a great shot it was. So thank-you again Mr Gilfoyle and I hope you will have a happy and blessed new year.

All the best

Pearce and Janelle

Brian Bullock comes from Launceston in Tasmania. Brian and his wife Margaret were staying at the Big Rig Van Park when they read about the saleyards and Brian decided to go and have a look.

I caught up with him during a store sale and he had this to say:

I've worked in the bush and I've been to cattle sales but nothing like this; I've never seen anything like this and I've never even imagined what 6,000 cattle in the yards all at once would look like.

It's all very impressive and Margaret is going to be very disappointed that she didn't come when I go back to the van and tell her the full story about all that goes on here.

To go and have a look at something like this is fantastic; not just the agents and the auctioneers, but the horsemen taking the cattle to the scales and then to see all those gates working by remote control and the cattle being weighed – you've gotta see it to believe it!

I met a couple of the locals: Bill Harris who owns a property, Glen Nielsen who is an agent, and also Jimmy Coleman one of the buyers. All terrific blokes to talk to and they made me feel part of it.

And as I was following the sale I saw a bloke buy five pens in one hit – 153 Poll Hereford steers from "Chippendale" at Blackall – and I worked it out they cost him about $750 a head, which is around $110,000 all up … and you suddenly realise this is really big business!

I was very interested in the trucks too; we don't have road trains in Tasmania so that was something else to experience close up.

I reckon the whole show is great and I'll be telling everyone we meet that a visit here is well worthwhile.

Bruce & Hilary McDonald were visiting Australia from South Canterbury NZ when they called in one Thursday to see the fat sale.

I asked them why they came here:

"Well we had a couple of days with Graham Curley at "Bendigo Park" Cloncurry," said Bruce. He told us about Roma Saleyards and recommended that we take the time to have a look.

Back home, we run sheep, cattle and deer and I'm on the Temuka Saleyards Board, so we were keen to come. We fly out from Brisbane tomorrow so we've just managed to squeeze it in.

We were interested to see how it all works and I was very impressed by the flow of cattle over the scales and the speed of the whole operation. We have weekly sales at Temuka, but nothing like this; it's been a real eye-opener."

"The efficiency of the staff impressed me," said Hilary. "Just watching from the platform, seeing the coordination of the whole selling process from the auctioneers right through to the scales and into the delivery pens, I thought it was all very orderly.

We met and spoke to one of the locals; he was good. He came and made himself known and explained how it all worked and that made it all so much the more interesting."

"That would be Barrie the Ambassador," I told them. "He used to be our Saleyards Board Chairman. He knows the place very well."

"It's been a great visit, we're so pleased we came and there are a lot of people in Kiwiland who will hear about it when we get back."

Michael & Pam Dransfield and **Peter & Anne Bennett** were travelling together from Palmerston North, New Zealand, when they called in to a store sale one Tuesday.

Before they left, I asked them what they thought of the place:

Most impressed; I've never seen saleyards as smart as these. It's all extremely well organised. And to think cattle come from such enormous distances; it's a credit to your cattle industry, it really is.

Also, you get a good cup of tea and a good cup of coffee here as well. It's a place we could happily recommend to our friends especially anyone off the land.

Ken Casperson is the artist who did the paintings in this book.

I met him by chance at Roma Saleyards when he was out from Brisbane looking for suitable subjects to paint. It turned out that Ken knew my father, Jack Gilfoyle, when they both worked for the Queensland Housing Commission, and so a new friendship developed.

In his working life, Ken was an Architectural Draftsperson and Landscape Architect. Now retired, he has adapted his professional training to painting and developed a unique style in watercolour composition that has impressed the critics.

Ken likes to go fishing at Caloundra but his work is in such demand that his painting is interfering with his fishing; in fact he's the only artist I've met who complains about too many orders.

Thanks for coming, Ken, and thanks for your invaluable contribution.

11. The Hammer's Up!

Yes, the hammer's up, it's had its time; let's call it a day.

The book is intended to bring back happy memories for those of you who know Roma Saleyards or knew it in the old days.

It is also designed to help those who have briefly visited the place to realise what makes it tick – the people!

For those of you who have never been here, never sold here, never bought here, or never paid us a visit, it is to be hoped what you have read will encourage you to come to here.

The book has one thing in common with the yards: there's not enough room. Not enough room to mention all the people who come here and sometimes not enough room for all the cattle that turn up.

In the fifties and sixties there were saleyards at Cunnamulla, Quilpie, Charleville (2), Mitchell, Injune, Roma (3), Wallumbilla (2), Yuleba, Dulacca (2), Miles, Wandoan, Taroom and Chinchilla.

Today Roma Saleyards is the only one left and thanks to the improvement in roads, double decker transports, and the continuing upgrading and extension of facilities, thousands of cattle pour in here every week. Sometimes there is just not enough room for them all.

So too with the book!

Cover to cover there are 224 pages, just over 500 people have been mentioned and nearly 700 have been photographed, but hundreds of others haven't … simply because there's not enough room.

In some cases, when cross referencing stories, you'll find that one version differs from the next, just as one person's recollections of the past differ from the other.

Who cares? Let not the truth stand in the way of a good story!

Neither is telling lies, the basic facts are the same, it's agreed the incident did occur, but just who was the culprit may remain a mystery, something to argue about when the footy season is over.

In closing, I must say putting this book together has been fun.

It has taught me a lot more about Roma Saleyards than I thought possible and it has introduced me to people from around Australia and all over the world. I have made new friends, had a lot of laughs and thoroughly enjoyed the experience.

And I hope you did too!

Index – The People

Gibbs, Reg & Beryl, 194
Gilfoyle, Jack, 206
Gilfoyle, John & Lurelle, 198
Gilfoyle, Lurelle, 107, 189
Gillespie, Bob, 160
Gleeson, Ben, 46
Gleeson, Dick, 118
Gleeson, Jack, 1
Golden, Amanda, 43, 50
Golden, Hal & Mary, 43
Goodhew, Steve, 132, 183, 186
Gould, Damian, 95
Gould, Lee, 95
Grace, Tom, 14, 23
Grace, Tom & Mary, 17
Graham, Doug, 199
Graham, Mavis, 83
Grant, Paul, 198
Green, Jim, 183, 185
Green, Peter, 7, 12
Greer, Gary, 110, 168
Grills, Jim, 155
Grills, Mick, 155
Guest & Co, 12
Guymer, Murray, 56

H

Hall, Bob, 25
Hann, Eileen, 80
Harland, Bob, 130, 174
Harland, Darryl, 162, 163, 183
Harland, Norm, 4, 158
Harms, Boyd, 171
Harms, Karl, 177
Harms, Ken, 85
Harms, Noel, 85
Harms, Rob, 73, 85
Harms, Robbie, 85
Harms, Roy, 4, 6, 36, 85
Harms, Val, 5, 6, 20, 52, 54, 78, 84, 85,
    100, 110, 120, 131, 133, 158, 160,
    163, 167, 179, 185
Harris, Bill, 205
Hartley, Bill, 31, 156
Hartley, John, 31
Hartley, Tom, 31
Harvey, Adrian, 94
Harvey, Grace, 77
Harvey, Tammy, 77
Hassett, Charlie, 155

Healy, Kevin, 76, 82, 91, 95, 122, 128,
    131, 134, 163, 171
Heelan, Doug, 104, 161, 171
Henderson, George, 5, 161, 162
Henderson, Graham, 196
Henderson, Judith, 160
Henning, Don, 35, 155, 160
Henry, Col, 95
Henry, Scott, 19
Hepburn, Alan, 155
Hickey, Bryan, 5, 6, 162, 168, 170
Hickey, Dennis, 11
Higgins, Joey, 32
Higgins, John, 162
Hinze, Russ, 15
Holland, Peter, 18, 84, 105, 130, 133,
    163, 179, 184, 186, 196
Holland, Travis, 186
Holland, Vicky, 133
Holt, Andrew, 186
Hooper, Bryce, 82
Howard, Peter, 112
Huddlestone, Roy, 161
Hughes, Barry, 186
Hughes, Garth, 32, 35, 159, 172, 178
Humphreys, Billy, 83
Humphris, Wally, 7, 104, 171
Hunt, Tom, 21
Hutton, Stuart, 132
Hyland, Terry, 128, 186

I

Innes, Don, 175
Isles, Bob, 4, 158
Isles, Bob & Bill, 157

J

Jensen, Andrew, 179, 181, 186
Jensen, Melissa, 20, 21, 76, 198, 200
Jensen, Melissa., 54
Jensen, Ron, 181
Johnson, Fergie, 161
Johnson, Ken, 11
Johnston, Gary, 99
Johnston, Gordon, 50, 55
Jones, Charlie, 168

K

Kadel, Charlie, 4
Kane, Ross, 162
Kavanagh, Ken, 4
Kay, Dave, 155
Kelly, Christie, 175
Kelly, Don, 130, 174, 186
Kennedy, Susie, 80
Keong, Fred, 122
Keppel, Joe, 129
Keppy, Roy, 155
Kidd, Sandy, 40
Kidman & Co, 12
Killen, Geoff, 105
Kimlin, Keith, 42, 47, 56, 78, 109, 190
Kinman, Malcolm, 171
Kirk, Doug, 9, 157, 164
Kitchen, Pat, 119
Klar, Paul, 73
Knaggs, Alban, 101
Knauer, Peter, 6, 40, 103, 131, 134, 158, 163, 171
Knott, Andrew, 196
Knott, Johanna, 196
Knott, Noeline, 196
Knott, Robert, 196
Knott, Thomas., 196
Knox, Sir William, 5
Krienke, Ken, 56, 73
Kruger, Daryl, 115
Kruger, Dexter, 114
Kruger, Dexter & Gladys, 114
Kruger, Gregory, 114
Kruger, Kruger, 201

L

Ladbrook, Gary & Kerry, 30
Ladbrook, George, 80
Lalor, Dudley, 155, 161
Lane, Don, 15
Lanskey, Terry, 26, 96
Latemore, Les, 28
Laws, John, 172
Lawton, Bill, 155, 158
Leaming, Dr., 38
Lehman, Lester, 156
Lenihan, Pat, 49, 76, 78
Lima, Paulo & Ana, 197
List, Colin, 199

Lister, Rob, 154
Lloyd, John, 94
Lloyd, Ron & Margaret, 197
Logan, Dorothy, 107, 165
Logan, Gerry, 7, 132
Logan, Wallace, 29, 32, 34, 40, 106, 122, 164
Loneragan, Tim, 155
Lord, Peter, 120
Loughnan, Barrie, 33, 77, 108, 188, 202, 206
Loughnan, Rob, 79, 188

M

Macallister, Ian & Joy, 35
Macca, 187
MacLaughlin, Hector, 179
Manser, George, 155
Martin, Alec, 93
Martyn, John, 41, 173
Maslen, Geoff, 178, 186
Matthews, Jim, 116, 183
Matthewson, John, 89
McCabe, Barry & Sue, 194
McCauley, Max, 190
McClymont, Malcolm, 12
McConnell, Nev, 166
McCormack, Paul, 81, 84, 112
McDonald, Bruce & Hilary, 205
McDonald, Peter, 186
McDougall, Ron, 155, 161
McFadzen, Graham & Jill, 201
McGrath, Ken, 5
McGuinn, Chad, 73, 87
McInnerney Brothers, 104
McIntosh, Neil, 22
McIntosh, Roy, 180
McIver, Bruce, 15
McKay, Barney, 104
McKay, Bill, 104
McKay, Dave, 56, 73
McLennan, Jack, 155
McLennan, Len, 155
McLennan, Tony, 92, 107
McLeod, Duncan, 167, 177, 186
McMahon, Frank, 118
McMahon, John, 82, 121, 171, 184
McMahon, Leo, 32
McMeniman, Tom, 155
McMillan, Don, 154

The Numbers

The numbers have continued to grow since new yards were constructed by the Board in 1969:

During the Seventies – 10 Years – 69/70 to 78/79

922,000 cattle sold to average 92,200 a year at $87/head.

During the Eighties – 10 Years – 79/80 to 88/89

1.47m cattle sold to average 147,400 a year at $233/head

	Number	Average	Gross
1989/90	165,569	$348.08	$ 57.6m
1990/91	176,870	$363.99	$ 64.4m
1991/92	188,589	$309.15	$ 58.3m
1992/93	263,491	$300.67	$ 79.2m
1993/94	201,611	$396.72	$ 79.9m
1994/95	204,377	$345.68	$ 70.6m
1995/96	179,883	$278.51	$ 50.1m
1996/97	188,273	$282.87	$ 53.3m
1997/98	194,296	$313.34	$ 60.9m
1998/99	212,019	$382.69	$ 81.1m
1999/00	245,586	$406.16	$ 99.7m
2000/01	259,418	$483.71	$125.5m
2001/02	282,724	$495.46	$140.1m
2002/03	374,780	$366.24	$137.3m
2003/04	359,298	$515.37	$185.2m
2004/05	408,464	$577.28	$235.8m
2005/06	376,550	$584.23	$220.0m
2006/07	348,988	$529.27	$184.7m

1969-2007 - Seven million cattle worth $2,425 million sold.